To any reader, this anthology offers
hours of inspiration and meditation. The
classics mingle with the works of the
contemporaries; East meets West; every kind
of faith and point of view is represented;
romanticism nudges patriotism; and touches
of hearty homespun rival the exalted raptures.

Here is a glorious legacy of religious verse.
Sample it, quote it, share it—and return to it
often. It is music in words; a treasury of
man's response to life and God.

The
TREASURY
of RELIGIOUS
VERSE

Compiled by Donald T. Kauffman

PITY, RELIGION HAS SO SELDOM FOUND
A SKILLFUL GUIDE INTO POETIC GROUND!
THE FLOWERS WOULD SPRING WHERE'ER SHE DEIGNED TO STRAY,
AND EVERY MUSE ATTEND HER ON HER WAY.

William Cowper

PILLAR BOOKS   NEW YORK

FOR
MY MOTHER
WHOSE FAITH SINGS

THE TREASURY OF RELIGIOUS VERSE

A PILLAR BOOK
Published by arrangement with the Fleming H. Revell Company

Second printing, January 1976

ISBN: 0-89129-081-8

Library of Congress Catalog Card Number: 62-10735

Printed in the United States of America

PILLAR BOOKS is a division of Pyramid Communications, Inc.
919 Third Avenue, New York, New York 10022, U.S.A.

ACKNOWLEDGMENTS

Special acknowledgment is made to the following who have granted permission for the privilege of including selections in this volume:

ABINGDON PRESS for "Sheer Joy" and "The Secret" from *Spiritual Hilltops,* copyright renewal 1960 by Ralph S. Cushman, and for "Love" from *Songs From the Slums* by Toyohiko Kagawa, copyright 1935 by Whitmore & Smith, copyright renewal 1963 by Lois J. Erickson. By permission of Abingdon Press.

ASSOCIATION PRESS for "O Young and Fearless Prophet" from *Prayers for Times Like These* by Ralph Harlow.

EDNA BECKER for "Reflections."

THE BOBBS-MERRILL COMPANY, INC. for "Away" by James Whitcomb Riley.

THE BRETHREN PRESS for "The Touch of the Master's Hand" by Myra Brooks Welch.

ELIZABETH DAVIS BURFORD for "We Bear the Strain of Earthly Care" by Ozora S. Davis.

BURNS & OATES LTD. for "I Am the Way" by Alice Meynell.

CAMBRIDGE UNIVERSITY PRESS and OXFORD UNIVERSITY PRESS for material from *The New English Bible* © The Delegates of the Oxford University Press and The Syndics of the Cambridge University Press, 1961.

CHAUTAUQUA INSTITUTION for "Day Is Dying in the West" by Mary A. Lathbury.

PEGGY POND CHURCH for "Ultimatum."

HAZEL DAVIS CLARK for "Apparitions" by Thomas Curtis Clark, and for "A Virile Christ" by Rex Boundy from *Christ in Poetry,* edited by Thomas Curtis Clark and Hazel Davis Clark, published by Association Press. Used by permission.

PHILIP JEROME CLEVELAND for "By Night," "I Yield Thee Praise," and "There Is a Love."

W. W. COBLENTZ for "The Housewife" by Catherine Cate Coblentz, published by Harper & Brothers.

CONCERN for "The Middle-Time" by Lona M. Fowler. Reprinted by permission of *Concern,* official magazine of United Presbyterian Women, and the author.

MYLES CONNOLLY for "Said the Innkeeper" and "Quo Vadis?"

PURD E. DEITZ for "Builders," copyright 1936, Purd E. Deitz. Used by permission.

DODD, MEAD & COMPANY for "Where Is Heaven?" reprinted by permission of Dodd, Mead & Company from *Bliss Carman's Poems* copyright 1929 by Bliss Carman; for "Home at Last" and "The Holy of Holies" reprinted by permission of Dodd, Mead & Company from *Collected Poems* by G. K. Chesterton; and for selection from "Rhymes of a Rolling Stone" from *Collected Poems of Robert Service* copyright 1912, 1939 by Robert W. Service.

DOUBLEDAY & CO. INC. for "The Job That's Crying To Be Done" from "The Glory of the Garden" © 1911 Rudyard Kipling from *Rudyard Kipling's Verse: Definitive Edition.*

MRS. WALTER DOUGLAS and CLARA LOUISE MOMENT for "The Best Treasure" by John J. Moment.

GEORGIA MOORE EBERLING for "The Centuries Are His."

MARY S. EDGAR for "The Camp Hymn."

LOIS J. ERICKSON for "Meditation" by Toyohiko Kagawa, interpreted by Lois J. Erickson.

EVANGELICAL PUBLISHERS for poems by Annie Johnson Flint. Copyright. Reproduced by permission. Evangelical Publishers, Toronto, Canada.

FABER AND FABER, LTD. for selection from *Holes in the Sky* by Louis Mac-Neice, published by Faber and Faber, Ltd.

FLORENCE KIPER FRANK for "The Jew to Jesus."

ETHEL ROMIG FULLER for "Proof."

WINFRED ERNEST GARRISON for "The Book."

PREFACE

Edwin Markham says of poetry:

> *She comes like the hush and beauty of the night,*
> *And sees too deep for laughter;*
> *Her touch is a vibration and a light*
> *From worlds before and after.*

In gathering the selections for this volume I have glimpsed that vision and felt that vibration, almost as one touching the invisible.

This is a treasury of poetry in many voices, from many times and places. There is a tremendous difference between the exalted raptures of William Wordsworth and the rollicking homespun of Robert Service or Edgar A. Guest, and the contrast of Francis Thompson's intricate images with the simple but equally devout song of Annie Johnson Flint is great. So is the gap between such widely separated poetic points as the serene faith of George Macdonald, the yearning melodies of Tennyson, the probing conscience of Edwin Markham, and the stinging satire of W. H. Auden and T. S. Eliot. Yet these and many other versifiers together reveal vistas of the heights and depths and outreaches of the Kingdom of God that enlarge the heart. . . .

. . . And warm the heart, too. In "The Old Hundredth" our fathers exulted,

> *Sing to the Lord with cheerful voice;*
> *Him serve with mirth, His praise forth tell,*
> *Come ye before Him, and rejoice!*

May all who read these selections experience something of the

compiler's delight in finding and arranging them, and be aga
and again "surprised by joy."

It is hoped that this anthology may provide treasures for tho
speakers and writers who mine here for telling quotations an
illustrations.

This book would not exist but for a host of individuals livin
and dead who have impressed upon me the indestructible bon
between poetry and faith. In particular, I wish to thank these: m
father and mother for introducing me early to good literature as we
as to good religion; Josephine Rickard for bringing me an apprec
ation of some of the classical masters of verse; Paul Scherer f
leading me to a deeper awareness of the religious message of certai
contemporary poets; my "father- and mother-in-love" for aid in th
compiling; and Frank S. Mead and Wilbur H. Davies for encou
aging the work. For the book's design and typography I would lik
to express appreciation to Arthur Michalez. And without the sym
pathy and good taste of my wife, *The Treasury of Religious Vers*
would be less complete.

Donald T. Kauffma

CONTENTS

V. THE REIGN OF GOD

I

GOD OF GLORY

1. All Nature Sings

THIS IS MY FATHER'S WORLD

This is my Father's world;
And to my listening ears,
All nature sings, and round me rings
The music of the spheres.
This is my Father's world;
I rest me in the thought
Of rocks and trees, of skies and seas,
His hand the wonders wrought.

This is my Father's world;
The birds their carols raise,
The morning light, the lily white,
Declare their Maker's praise.
This is my Father's world;
He shines in all that's fair;
In the rustling grass I hear him pass;
He speaks to me everywhere.

This is my Father's world;
Oh, let me ne'er forget
That though the wrong seems oft so strong,
God is the ruler yet.
This is my Father's world;
Why should my heart be sad?
The Lord is king; let the heavens ring.
God reigns; let the earth be glad.

Maltbie D. Babcock

PIPPA'S SONG

The year's at the spring,
And day's at the morn;
Morning's at seven;
The hill-side's dew-pearl'd;
The lark's on the wing;
The snail's on the thorn;
God's in His heaven—
All's right with the world!

Robert Browning

MY HEART LEAPS UP

My heart leaps up when I behold
    A rainbow in the sky;
So was it when my life began;
So is it now I am a man;
So be it when I shall grow old.
    Or let me die!
The Child is father of the Man;
And I could wish my days to be
Bound each to each by natural piety.

William Wordsworth

FROM SONG OF MYSELF

I believe a leaf of grass is no less than the journey-work of the stars,
And the pismire is equally perfect, and a grain of sand,
        and the egg of the wren,
And the tree-toad is a chef-d'oeuvre for the highest,
And the running blackberry would adorn the parlors of heaven,
And the narrowest hinge in my hand puts to scorn all machinery,
And the cow crunching with depress'd head surpasses any statue,
And a mouse is miracle enough to stagger sextillions of infidels.

Walt Whitman

MY GARDEN

A garden is a lovesome thing, God wot!
   Rose plot,
Fringed pool,
Fern'd grot—
   The veriest school
   Of peace; and yet the fool
Contends that God is not—
Not God! in gardens! when the eve is cool?
   Nay, but I have a sign;
   'Tis very sure God walks in mine.

Thomas Edward Brown

THE HOLY OF HOLIES

"Elder Father, though thine eyes
   Shine with hoary mysteries,
   Canst thou tell what in the heart
   Of a cowslip blossom lies?"

"Smaller than all lives that be,
   Secret as the deepest sea,
   Stands a little house of seeds
   Like an elfin's granary."

"Speller of the stones and weeds
   Skilled in Nature's crafts and creeds,
   Tell me what is in the heart
   Of the smallest of the seeds."

"God Almighty, and with Him
   Cherubim and Seraphim,
   Filling all eternity,
   Adonai Elohim!"

G. K. Chesterton

FROM *ENDYMION*

A thing of beauty is a joy for ever:
Its loveliness increases; it will never
Pass into nothingness; but still will keep
A bower quiet for us, and a sleep
Full of sweet dreams, and health, and quiet breathing. . . .
An endless fountain of immortal drink,
Pouring unto us from the heaven's brink.

John Keats

A PRAYER

Teach me, Father, how to go
Softly as the grasses grow;
Hush my soul to meet the shock
Of the wild world as a rock;
But my spirit, propt with power,
Make as simple as a flower.
Let the dry heart fill its cup,
Like a poppy looking up;
Let life lightly wear her crown,
Like a poppy looking down,
When its heart is filled with dew,
And its life begins anew.

Teach me, Father, how to be
Kind and patient as a tree.
Joyfully the crickets croon
Under shady oak at noon;
Beetle, on his mission bent,
Tarries in that cooling tent.
Let me, also, cheer a spot,
Hidden field or garden grot—
Place where passing souls can rest
On the way and be their best.

Edwin Markham

FROM *RULES AND LESSONS*

Observe God in His works: here fountains flow,
   Birds sing, beasts feed, fish leap, and th' Earth stands fast:
Above are restless motions, running lights,
Vast circling azure, giddy clouds, days, nights.

Henry Vaughan

THE HIGHER PANTHEISM

The sun, the moon, the stars, the seas,
     the hills and the plains,—
Are not these, O Soul, the Vision of Him, who reigns?

Is not the Vision He, tho' He be not that which He seems?
Dreams are true while they last, and do we not live in dreams?

Earth, these solid stars, this weight of body and limb,
Are they not sign and symbol of thy division from Him?

Dark is the world to thee; thyself art the reason why,
For is He not all but thou, that hast power to feel "I am I"?

Glory about thee, without thee; and thou fulfillest thy doom,
Making Him broken gleams and a stifled splendor and gloom.

Speak to Him, thou, for He hears, and Spirit
     with Spirit can meet—
Closer is He than breathing, and nearer than hands and feet.

God is law, say the wise; O Soul, and let us rejoice,
For if He thunder by law the thunder is yet His voice.

Law is God, say some; no God at all, says the fool,
For all we have power to see is a straight staff bent in a pool;

And the ear of man cannot hear, and the eye of man cannot see;
But if we could see and hear, this Vision—were it not He?

Alfred Tennyson

HIGH FLIGHT

Oh! I have slipped the surly bonds of earth
  And danced the skies on laughter-silvered wings;
Sunward I've climbed, and joined the tumbling mirth
  Of sun-split clouds—and done a hundred things
You have not dreamed of—wheeled and soared and swung
  High in the sunlit silence. Hov'ring there,
I've chased the shouting wind along, and flung
  My eager craft through footless halls of air.

Up, up the long, delirious, burning blue
  I've topped the wind-swept heights with easy grace
Where never lark, or even eagle flew—
  And, while with silent lifting mind I've trod
The high untrespassed sanctity of space,
  Put out my hand and touched the face of God.

Pilot Officer John Gillespie Magee, Jr., R.C.A.F.

AT LITTLE VIRGIL'S WINDOW

There are three green eggs in a small brown pocket,
And the breeze will swing and the gale will rock it,
Till three little birds on the thin edge teeter,
And our God be glad and our world be sweeter!

Edwin Markham

8

WHEN I HEARD THE LEARN'D ASTRONOMER

When I heard the learn'd astronomer:
When the proofs, the figures, were ranged in columns before me;
When I was shown the charts and diagrams, to add, divide, and
    measure them;
When I, sitting, heard the astronomer, where he lectured
    with much applause in the lecture-room,
How soon, unaccountable, I became tired and sick;
Till rising and gliding out, I wander'd off by myself,
In the mystical moist night-air, and from time to time,
Look'd up in perfect silence at the stars.

Walt Whitman

THE RHODORA

In May, when sea-winds pierced our solitudes,
I found the fresh Rhodora in the woods,
Spreading its leafless blooms in a damp nook,
To please the desert and the sluggish brook.
The purple petals, fallen in the pool,
Made the black water with their beauty gay;
Here might the red-bird come his plumes to cool,
And court the flower that cheapens his array.
Rhodora! if the sages ask thee why
This charm is wasted on the earth and sky,
Tell them, dear, that if eyes were made for seeing,
Then Beauty is its own excuse for being:
Why wert thou there, O rival of the rose!
I never thought to ask, I never knew;
But, in my simple ignorance, suppose
The self-same Power that brought me there brought you.

Ralph Waldo Emerson

THE DAY RETURNS

The day returns
And brings us the petty round
Of irritating concerns and duties.
Help us to play the man!
Help us to perform them
With laughter and kind faces.
Let cheerfulness abound with industry.
Give us to go blithely on our business
All this day.
Bring us to our resting beds
Weary, and content,
And undishonored,
And grant us in the end
The gift of sleep. Amen.

Robert Louis Stevenson

THE CAMP HYMN

God, who touchest earth with beauty,
  Make me lovely too;
With Thy Spirit re-create me,
  Make my heart anew.

Like Thy springs and running waters,
  Make me crystal pure;
Like Thy rocks of towering grandeur,
  Make me strong and sure.

Like Thy dancing waves in sunlight,
  Make me glad and free;
Like the straightness of the pine trees
  Let me upright be.

Like the arching of the heavens,
    Lift my thoughts above;
Turn my dreams to noble action—
    Ministries of love.

God, who touchest earth with beauty,
    Make me lovely too;
Keep me ever, by Thy Spirit,
    Pure and strong and true.

Mary S. Edgar

FLOWER IN THE CRANNIED WALL

Flower in the crannied wall,
I pluck you out of the crannies,
I hold you here, root and all, in my hand,
Little flower—but *if* I could understand
What you are, root and all, and all in all,
I should know what God and man is.

Alfred Tennyson

FROM *AURORA LEIGH*

Earth's crammed with heaven,
And every common bush afire with God;
    But only he who sees, takes off his shoes,
    The rest sit round it and pluck blackberries,
    And daub their natural faces unaware
    More and more from the first similitude.

Elizabeth Barrett Browning

DAWN

Out of the scabbard of the night
  By God's hand drawn,
Flashes his shining sword of light,
  And lo—the dawn!

Frank Dempster Sherman

MYSTERIES

The murmur of a bee
A witchcraft yieldeth me.
If any ask me why,
'Twere easier to die
Than tell.

The red upon the hill
Taketh away my will;
If anybody sneer,
Take care, for God is here,
That's all.

The breaking of the day
Addeth to my degree;
If any ask me how,
Artist, who drew me so,
Must tell!

Emily Dickinson

OUT IN THE FIELDS WITH GOD

The little cares that fretted me,
  I lost them yesterday,
Among the fields above the sea,
  Among the winds at play,
Among the lowing of the herds,

> The rustling of the trees,
> Among the singing of the birds,
> The humming of the bees.

> The foolish fears of what might pass
>   I cast them all away
> Among the clover-scented grass
>   Among the new-mown hay,
> Among the rustling of the corn
>   Where drowsy poppies nod,
> Where ill thoughts die and good are born—
>   Out in the fields with God!

Author unknown

GOD IS AT THE ANVIL

God is at the anvil, beating out the sun:
Where the molten metal spills,
At his forge among the hills,
He has hammered out the glory of a day that's done.

God is at the anvil, welding golden bars:
In the scarlet streaming flame,
He is fashioning a frame
For the shimmering silver beauty of the evening stars.

Lew Sarett

FROM *THE DIVINE COMEDY*

I raised my eyes aloft, and I beheld
The scattered chapters of the Universe
Gathered and bound into a single book
By the austere and tender hand of God.

Dante Alighieri

WIND IN THE PINE

Oh, I can hear you, God, above the cry
    Of the tossing trees—
Rolling your windy tides across the sky,
    And splashing your silver seas
        Over the pine,
        To the water-line
        Of the moon.
      Oh, I can hear you, God,
Above the wail of the lonely loon—
When the pine-tops pitch and nod—
    Chanting your melodies
Of ghostly waterfalls and avalanches,
Washing your wind among the branches
    To make them pure and white.
Wash over me, God, with your piney breeze
    And your moon's wet-silver pool;
Wash over me, God, with your wind and night,
    And leave me clean and cool.

Lew Sarett

HYACINTHS TO FEED THY SOUL

If of thy mortal goods thou art bereft,
And from thy slender store two loaves alone
    to thee are left,
Sell one, and with the dole
Buy hyacinths to feed thy soul.

Gulistan of Moslih Eddin Saadi

DAY IS DYING IN THE WEST

Day is dying in the west;
Heaven is touching earth with rest;

Wait and worship while the night
Sets her evening lamps alight
Through all the sky.
Holy, holy, holy, Lord God of Hosts!
Heaven and earth are full of thee!

Lord of life, beneath the dome
Of the universe, thy home,
Gather us who seek thy face
To the fold of thy embrace,
For thou art nigh.
Holy, holy, holy, Lord God of Hosts!
Heaven and earth are full of thee!

When forever from our sight
Pass the stars, the day, the night,
Lord of angels, on our eyes
Let eternal morning rise,
And shadows end.
Holy, holy, holy, Lord God of Hosts!
Heaven and earth are full of thee!

Mary A. Lathbury

THE UNKNOWN GOD

The Lord hath builded for Himself
  He needs no earthly dome;
The universe His dwelling is,
  Eternity His home.

Yon glorious sky His temple stands,
  So lofty, bright, and blue,
All lamped with stars, and curtained round
  With clouds of every hue.

Earth is His altar: Nature there
   Her daily tribute pays;
The elements upon Him wait;
   The seasons roll His praise.

Where shall I see Him? How describe
   The Dread, Eternal One?
His foot-prints are in every place,
   Himself is found in none.

He called the world, and it arose;
   The heavens, and they appeared:
His hand poured forth the mighty deep;
   His arm the mountains reared.

He sets His foot upon the hills,
   And earth beneath Him quakes;
He walks upon the hurricane,
   And in the thunder speaks.

I search the rounds of space and time,
   Nor find His semblance there:
Grandeur has nothing so sublime,
   Nor Beauty half so fair.

Henry Francis Lyte

FROM *AUGURIES OF INNOCENCE*

To see a World in a Grain of Sand
And a Heaven in a Wild Flower,
Hold Infinity in the palm of your hand
And Eternity in an hour.

William Blake

16

TO THE EVENING STAR

Star that bringest home the bee,
And sett'st the weary labourer free!
If any star shed peace, 'tis Thou
    That send'st it from above.
Appearing when Heaven's breath and brow
    Are sweet as hers we love.

Come to the luxuriant skies,
Whilst the landscape's odours rise,
Whilst far-off lowing herds are heard
    And songs when toil is done,
From cottages whose smoke unstirr'd
    Curls yellow in the sun.

Star of love's soft interviews,
Parted lovers on thee muse;
Their remembrancer in Heaven
    Of thrilling vows thou art,
Too delicious to be riven
    By absence from the heart.

Thomas Campbell

THE TIGER

Tiger, tiger, burning bright
In the forests of the night,
What immortal hand or eye
Could frame thy fearful symmetry?

In what distant deeps or skies
Burnt the fire of thine eyes?
On what wings dare he aspire?
What the hand dare seize the fire?

17

And what shoulder and what art
Could twist the sinews of thy heart?
And, when thy heart began to beat,
What dread hand and what dread feet?

What the hammer? What the chain?
In what furnace was thy brain?
What the anvil? What dread grasp
Dare its deadly terrors clasp?

When the stars threw down their spears,
And water'd heaven with their tears,
Did He smile His work to see?
Did He who made the lamb make thee?

Tiger, tiger, burning bright
In the forests of the night,
What immortal hand or eye
Dare frame thy fearful symmetry?

William Blake

THE MANUSCRIPTS OF GOD

And nature, the old nurse, took
   The child upon her knee,
Saying, "Here is a story book
   My father hath writ for thee.
Come, wander with me," she said,
   "In regions yet untrod
And read what is still unread
   In the manuscripts of God."

Henry Wadsworth Longfellow

BY THE SEA

It is a beauteous evening, calm and free;
The holy time is quiet as a Nun
Breathless with adoration; the broad sun
Is sinking down in its tranquillity;
The gentleness of heaven broods o'er the Sea:
Listen! the mighty Being is awake,
And doth with his eternal motion make
A sound like thunder—everlastingly.
Dear Child! dear Girl! that walkest with me here,
If thou appear untouch'd by solemn thought
Thy nature is not therefore less divine:
Thou liest in Abraham's bosom all the year,
And worshipp'st at the Temple's inner shrine,
God being with thee when we know it not.

William Wordsworth

NATURE

As a fond mother, when the day is o'er,
　Leads by the hand her little child to bed,
　Half willing, half reluctant to be led,
　And leave his broken playthings on the floor,
Still gazing at them through the open door,
　Nor wholly reassured and comforted
　By promises of others in their stead,
　Which, though more splendid, may not please him more;
So Nature deals with us, and takes away
　Our playthings one by one, and by the hand
　Leads us to rest so gently, that we go
Scarce knowing if we wish to go or stay,
　Being too full of sleep to understand
　How far the unknown transcends the what we know.

Henry Wadsworth Longfellow

19

2. The Divine Presence

TO GOD

Lord, I am like the mistletoe,
Which has no root and cannot grow
Or prosper, but by that same tree
It clings about: so I by Thee.
What need I then to fear at all
So long as I about Thee crawl?
But if that tree should fall and die,
Tumble shall heaven, and so down will I.

Robert Herrick

BY THY LIFE I LIVE

I love, my God, but with no love of mine,
    For I have none to give;
I love Thee, Lord, but all the love is Thine,
    For by Thy life I live.
I am as nothing, and rejoice to be
Emptied and lost and swallowed up in Thee.

Thou, Lord, alone art all Thy children need,
    And there is none beside;
From Thee the streams of blessedness proceed;
    In Thee the blest abide,
Fountain of life, and all-abounding grace,
Our source, our center, and our dwelling place!

Madame Jeanne Marie Guyon

THE SECRET

I met God in the morning
    When my day was at its best,
And His presence came like sunrise,
    Like a glory in my breast.

All day long the Presence lingered,
    All day long He stayed with me,
And we sailed in perfect calmness
    O'er a very troubled sea.

Other ships were blown and battered,
    Other ships were sore distressed,
But the winds that seemed to drive them
    Brought to us a peace and rest.

Then I thought of other mornings,
    With a keen remorse of mind,
When I too had loosed the moorings,
    With the Presence left behind.

So I think I know the secret,
    Learned from many a troubled way:
You must seek Him in the morning
    If you want Him through the day!

Ralph Spaulding Cushman

"GIVE US THIS DAY OUR DAILY BREAD"

Back of the loaf is the snowy flour,
    And back of the flour the mill,
And back of the mill is the wheat and the
    shower,
And the sun and the Father's will.

Maltbie D. Babcock

21

FROM *TINTERN ABBEY*

I have learned
To look on nature, not as in the hour
Of thoughtless youth; but hearing oftentimes
The still, sad music of humanity,
Nor harsh, nor grating, though of ample power
To chasten and subdue. And I have felt
A presence that disturbs me with the joy
Of elevated thoughts; a sense sublime
Of something far more deeply interfused,
Whose dwelling is the light of setting suns,
And the round ocean and the living air,
And the blue sky, and in the mind of man;
A motion and a spirit, that impels
All thinking things, all objects of all thought,
And rolls through all things. Therefore am I still
A lover of the meadows and the woods,
And mountains; and of all that we behold
From this green earth; of all the mighty world
Of eye, and ear,—both what they half create,
And what perceive; well pleased to recognize
In nature and the language of the sense,
The anchor of my purest thoughts, the nurse,
The guide, the guardian of my heart, and soul
Of all my moral being.

William Wordsworth

FRAGMENT

Walk with thy fellow-creatures: note the hush
And whispers among them. There is not a spring
Or leaf but hath his morning hymn; each bush
And oak doth know I AM. Canst thou not sing?
   O leave thy cares and follies! go this way,
   And thou art sure to prosper all the day.

Henry Vaughan

WHERE IS HEAVEN?

Where is Heaven? Is it not
Just a friendly garden plot,
Walled with stone and roofed with sun,
Where the days pass one by one
Not too fast and not too slow,
Looking backward as they go
At the beauties left behind
To transport the pensive mind.

Does not Heaven begin that day
When the eager heart can say,
Surely God is in this place,
I have seen Him face to face,
In the loveliness of flowers,
In the service of the showers,
And His voice has talked to me
In the sunlit apple tree.

Bliss Carman

BEGIN THE DAY WITH GOD

Every morning lean thine arms awhile
Upon the window sill of heaven
And gaze upon thy Lord.
Then, with the vision in thy heart,
Turn strong to meet thy day.

Author unknown

TAKE MY HEART

Take my heart! for I cannot give it Thee:
Keep it! for I cannot keep it for Thee.

St. Augustine of Hippo

OMNIPRESENCE

A thousand sounds, and each a joyful sound;
The dragon flies are humming as they please,
The humming birds are humming all around,
The clithra all alive with buzzing bees,
Each playful leaf its separate whisper found,
As laughing winds went rustling through the grove;
And I saw thousands of such sights as these,
And heard a thousand sounds of joy and love.

And yet so dull I was, I did not know
That He was there who all this love displayed,
I did not think how He who loved us so
Shared all my joy, was glad that I was glad;
And all because I did not hear the word
In English accents say, "It is the Lord."

Edward Everett Hale

LOST AND FOUND

I missed him when the sun began to bend;
I found him not when I had lost his rim;
With many tears I went in search of him,
Climbing high mountains which did still ascend,
And gave me echoes when I called my friend;
Through cities vast and charnel-houses grim,
And high cathedrals where the light was dim,
Through books and arts and works without an end,
But found him not—the friend whom I had lost.
And yet I found him—as I found the lark,
A sound in fields I heard but could not mark;
I found him nearest when I missed him most;
I found him in my heart, a life in frost,
A light I knew not till my soul was dark.

George Macdonald

24

HYMN

When storms arise
And dark'ning skies
    About me threat'ning lower,
To Thee, O Lord, I raise mine eyes,
To Thee my tortured spirit flies
    For solace in that hour.

Thy mighty arm
Will let no harm
    Come near me nor befall me;
Thy voice shall quiet my alarm,
When life's great battle waxeth warm—
    No foeman shall appall me.

Upon Thy breast
Secure I rest
    From sorrow and vexation;
No more by sinful cares oppressed,
But in Thy presence ever blest,
    O God of my salvation.

                    Paul Laurence Dunbar

LINES WRITTEN IN HER BREVIARY

Let nothing disturb thee,
Nothing affright thee;
All things are passing;
God never changeth;
Patient endurance
Attaineth to all things;
Who God possesseth
In nothing is wanting;
Alone God sufficeth.

                St. Theresa (translated by
                Henry Wadsworth Longfellow)

ROUND OUR RESTLESSNESS

Oh, the little birds sang east, and the little birds sang west,
And I smiled to think God's greatness flowed
    around our incompleteness,—
Round our restlessness, his rest.

Elizabeth Barrett Browning

THE HANDIWORK OF GOD

I believe in the brook as it wanders
    From hillside into glade;
I believe in the breeze as it whispers
    When evening's shadows fade.
I believe in the roar of the river
    As it dashes from high cascade;
I believe in the cry of the tempest
    'Mid the thunder's cannonade.
I believe in the light of shining stars,
    I believe in the sun and the moon;
I believe in the flash of lightning,
    I believe in the night-bird's croon.
I believe in the faith of the flowers,
    I believe in the rock and sod,
For in all of these appeareth clear
    The handiwork of God.

Author unknown

WINGS

Let us be like a bird for a moment perched
    On a frail branch while he sings;
Though he feels it bend, yet he sings his song,
    Knowing that he has wings.

Victor Hugo

26

OUR BURDEN BEARER

The little sharp vexations
    And the briars that cut the feet,
Why not take all to the Helper
    Who has never failed us yet?
Tell Him about the heartache,
    And tell Him the longings too,
Tell Him the baffled purpose
    When we scarce know what to do.
Then, leaving all our weakness
    With the One divinely strong,
Forget that we bore the burden
    And carry away the song.

Phillips Brooks

MILTON'S PRAYER FOR PATIENCE

I am old and blind!
Men point at me as smitten by God's frown:
Afflicted and deserted of my kind,
    Yet am I not cast down.

I am weak, yet strong;
I murmur not that I no longer see;
Poor, old, and helpless, I the more belong,
    Father supreme, to Thee!

All-merciful One!
When men are furthest, then art Thou most near;
When friends pass by, my weaknesses to shun,
    Thy chariot I hear.

Thy glorious face
Is leaning toward me; and its holy light
Shines in upon my lonely dwelling place,—
    And there is no more night.

27

On my bended knee
I recognize Thy purpose clearly shown:
My vision Thou hast dimmed, that I may see
    Thyself, Thyself alone.

I have naught to fear;
This darkness is the shadow of Thy wing;
Beneath it I am almost sacred; here
    Can come no evil thing.

Oh, I seem to stand
Trembling, where foot of mortal ne'er hath been,
Wrapt in that radiance from the sinless land,
    Which eye hath never seen!

Visions come and go:
Shapes of resplendent beauty around me throng;
From angel lips I seem to hear the flow
    Of soft and holy song.

It is nothing now,
When heaven is opening on my sightless eyes,
When airs from Paradise refresh my brow,
    That earth in darkness lies.

In a purer clime
My being fills with rapture,—waves of thought
Roll in upon my spirit,—strains sublime
    Break over me unsought.

Give me now my lyre!
I feel the stirrings of a gift divine:
Within my bosom glows unearthly fire,
    Lit by no skill of mine.

Elizabeth Lloyd Howell

WHAT GOD HATH PROMISED

God hath not promised
  Skies always blue,
Flower-strewn pathways
  All our lives through;
God hath not promised
  Sun without rain,
Joy without sorrow,
  Peace without pain.

But God hath promised
  Strength for the day,
Rest for the labor,
  Light for the way,
Grace for the trials,
  Help from above,
Unfailing sympathy,
  Undying love.

Annie Johnson Flint

AFTER ST. AUGUSTINE

Sunshine let it be or frost,
  Storm or calm, as Thou shalt choose;
Though Thine every gift were lost,
  Thee Thyself we could not lose.

Mary Elizabeth Coleridge

THE ANCIENT THOUGHT

The round moon hangs like a yellow lantern in the trees
That lie like lace against the sky,
Oh, still the night! Oh, hushed the breeze—
  Surely God is nigh.

Watson Kerr

THE SHEPHERD BOY'S SONG

He that is down needs fear no fall,
  He that is low, no pride;
He that is humble ever shall
  Have God to be his guide.

I am content with that I have,
  Little be it or much;
And Lord, contentment still I crave,
  Because Thou savest such.

Fullness to such a burden is
  That go on pilgrimage;
Here little, and hereafter bliss,
  Is best from age to age.

John Bunyan

A PRAYER

Through every minute of this day,
  Be with me, Lord!
Through every day of all this week,
  Be with me, Lord!
Through every week of all this year,
  Be with me, Lord!

So shall the days and weeks and years
  Be threaded on a golden cord,
And all draw on with sweet accord
  Unto Thy fullness, Lord;
  That so, when time is past,
By grace I may at last
  Be with Thee, Lord!

John Oxenham

ARIDITY

O soul, canst thou not understand
Thou art not left alone,
As a dog to howl and moan
His master's absence? Thou art as a book
Left in a room that He forsook,
But returns to by and by,
A book of His dear choice,—
That quiet waiteth for His Hand,
That quiet waiteth for His Eye,
That quiet waiteth for His Voice.

Michael Field

FROM *AT THE END OF THINGS*

Cast away fear;
Be of good cheer;
He is here,
Is here!

Arthur Edward Waite

SUNRISE

Though the midnight found us weary,
    The morning brings us cheer;
Thank God for every sunrise
    In the circuit of the year.

Margaret E. Sangster

OUR HELP

Our help is in the name of the Lord,
Who made heaven and earth.

Psalm 124:8

THE SHADOWS

My little boy, with pale, round cheeks,
    And large, brown, dreamy eyes,
Not often, little wisehead, speaks,
    But yet will make replies.

His sister, always glad to show
    Her knowledge, for its praise,
Said yesterday: "God's here, you know;
    He's everywhere, always.

"He's in this room." His large, brown eyes
    Went wandering round for God;
In vain he looks, in vain he tries,
    His wits are all abroad.

"He is not here, mama? No, no;
    I do not see Him at all,
He's not the shadows, is He?" So
    His doubtful accents fall.

Fall on my heart, like precious seed,
    Grow up to flowers of love;
For as my child, in love and need,
    Am I to Him above.

How oft before the vapors break,
    And day begins to be,
In our dim-lighted rooms we take
    The shadows, Lord, for Thee;—

While every shadow lying there,
    Slow remnant of the night,
Is but an aching, longing prayer,
    For Thee, O Lord, the light.

George Macdonald

3. God's Love and Mercy

THE LORD'S MY SHEPHERD

The Lord's my shepherd, I'll not want;
He makes me down to lie
In pastures green; he leadeth me
The quiet waters by.

My soul he doth restore again;
And me to walk doth make
Within the paths of righteousness,
E'en for his own name's sake.

Yea, though I walk in death's dark vale,
Yet will I fear no ill,
For thou art with me, and thy rod
And staff me comfort still.

My table thou hast furnished
In presence of my foes;
My head thou dost with oil anoint,
And my cup overflows.

Goodness and mercy all my life
Shall surely follow me;
And in God's house for evermore
My dwelling place shall be.

Scottish Psalter

ON THE TWENTY-THIRD PSALM

In "pastures green"? Not always; sometimes He
Who knoweth best, in kindness leadeth me
In weary ways, where heavy shadows be.

And by "still waters"? No, not always so;
Oft times the heavy tempests round me blow,
And o'er my soul the waves and billows go.

But when the storm beats loudest, and I cry
Aloud for help, the Master standeth by,
And whispers to my soul, "Lo, it is I."

So, where He leads me, I can safely go,
And in the blest hereafter I shall know,
Why, in His wisdom, He hath led me so.

Author unknown

COMFORT

Speak low to me, my Saviour, low and sweet
From out the hallelujahs, sweet and low,
Lest I should fear and fall, and miss Thee so,
Who art not missed by any that entreat.
Speak to me as to Mary at Thy feet!
And if no precious gums my hands bestow,
Let my tears drop like amber, while I go
In reach of Thy divinest voice complete
In humanest affection—thus, in sooth,
To lose the sense of losing. As a child,
Whose song-bird seeks the wood for evermore,
Is sung to in its stead by mother's mouth,
Till, sinking on her breast, love-reconciled,
He sleeps the faster that he wept before.

Elizabeth Barrett Browning

34

LOVE

Love bade me welcome; yet my soul drew back,
　　Guilty of dust and sin.
But quick-eyed Love, observing me grow slack
　　From my first entrance in,
Drew nearer to me, sweetly questioning
　　If I lacked any thing.

"A guest," I answered, "worthy to be here."
　　Love said, "You shall be he."
"I, the unkind, ungrateful? Ah, my dear,
　　I cannot look on thee."
Love took my hand and smiling did reply,
　　"Who made the eyes but I?"

"Truth, Lord, but I have marred them; let my shame
　　Go where it doth deserve."
"And know you not," says Love, "who bore the blame?"
　　"My dear, then I will serve."
"You must sit down," says Love, "and taste my meat."
　　So I did sit and eat.

George Herbert

FROM *THE ETERNAL GOODNESS*

I see the wrong that round me lies,
　　I feel the guilt within;
I hear, with groan and travail-cries,
　　The world confess its sin.

Yet, in the maddening maze of things,
　　And tossed by storm and flood,
To one fixed trust my spirit clings:
　　I know that God is good!

John Greenleaf Whittier

35

THE ALL-EMBRACING

There's a wideness in God's mercy,
　Like the wideness of the sea;
There's a kindness in His justice,
　Which is more than liberty.

There is welcome for the sinner,
　And more graces for the good;
There is mercy with the Saviour;
　There is healing in His blood.

For the love of God is broader
　Than the measure of man's mind;
And the heart of the Eternal
　Is most wonderfully kind.

If our love were but more simple,
　We should take Him at His word;
And our lives would be all sunshine
　In the sweetness of our Lord.

Frederick W. Faber

THE TOYS

My little Son, who look'd from thoughtful eyes
And moved and spoke in quiet grown-up wise,
Having my law the seventh time disobey'd,
I struck him, and dismiss'd
With hard words and unkiss'd,
—His Mother, who was patient, being dead.
Then, fearing lest his grief should hinder sleep,
I visited his bed,
But found him slumbering deep,
With darken'd eyelids, and their lashes yet
From his late sobbing wet.

And I, with moan,
Kissing away his tears, left others of my own;
For, on a table drawn beside his head,
He had put, within his reach,
A box of counters and a red-vein'd stone,
A piece of glass abraded by the beach
And six or seven shells,
A bottle with bluebells,
And two French copper coins, ranged there with careful art,
To comfort his sad heart.
So when that night I pray'd
To God, I wept, and said:
Ah, when at last we lie with trancèd breath,
Not vexing Thee in death,
And thou rememberest of what toys
We made our joys,
How weakly understood,
Thy great commanded good,
Then, fatherly not less
Than I whom thou hast moulded from the clay,
Thou'lt leave Thy wrath, and say,
"I will be sorry for their childishness."

Coventry Patmore

OUT OF THE VAST

There's part of the sun in an apple,
    There's part of the moon in a rose;
There's part of the flaming Pleiades
    In every leaf that grows.
Out of the vast comes nearness;
    For the God whose love we sing
Lends a little of his heaven
    To every living thing.

Augustus Wright Bamberger

CONSIDER

Consider
The lilies of the field, whose bloom is brief—
We are as they;
Like them we fade away,
As doth a leaf.

Consider
The sparrows of the air, of small account:
Our God doth view
Whether they fall or mount—
He guards us too.

Consider
The lilies, that do neither spin nor toil,
Yet are most fair—
What profits all this care,
And all this coil?

Consider
The birds, that have no barn nor harvest-weeks:
God gives them food—
Much more our Father seeks
To do us good.

Christina Rossetti

GOD'S GARDEN

The years are flowers and bloom within
Eternity's wide garden;
The rose for joy, the thorn for sin,
The gardener, God, to pardon
All wilding growths, to prune, reclaim,
And make them rose-like in His name.

Richard Burton

HE GIVETH MORE

He giveth more grace when the burdens grow greater,
　He sendeth more strength when the labors increase;
To added affliction He addeth mercy,
　To multiplied trials, His multiplied peace.

When we have exhausted our store of endurance,
　When our strength has failed ere the day is half done,
When we reach the end of our hoarded resources,
　Our Father's full giving is only begun.

His love has no limit, His grace has no measure,
　His power no boundary known unto men;
For out of his infinite riches in Jesus
　He giveth and giveth and giveth again.

Annie Johnson Flint

I SOUGHT THE LORD

I sought the Lord, and afterward I knew
He moved my soul to seek Him, seeking me;
It was not I that found, O Saviour true,
No, I was found of Thee.

Thou didst reach forth Thy hand and mine enfold;
I walked and sank not on the storm-vexed sea,—
'Twas not so much that I on Thee took hold,
As Thou, dear Lord, on me.

I find, I walk, I love, but, O the whole
Of love is but my answer, Lord, to Thee:
For Thou wert long beforehand with my soul,
Always Thou lovedst me.

Author unknown

HOW GENTLE GOD'S COMMANDS

How gentle God's commands,
How kind his precepts are!
Come, cast your burdens on the Lord,
And trust his constant care.

While providence supports,
Let saints securely dwell;
That hand which bears all nature up
Shall guide his children well.

Why should this anxious load
Press down your weary mind?
Haste to your heavenly Father's throne,
And sweet refreshment find.

His goodness stands approved,
Down to the present day;
I'll drop my burden at his feet,
And bear a song away.

Philip Doddridge

FROM *AN EPISTLE*

So, the All-Great, were the All-Loving too—
So, through the thunder comes a human voice
Saying, "O heart I made, a heart beats here!
Face, my hands fashioned, see it in myself!
Thou hast no power nor mayst conceive of mine,
But love I gave thee, with myself to love,
And thou must love me who have died for thee!"

Robert Browning

LET US WITH A GLADSOME MIND

Let us with a gladsome mind
Praise the Lord, for he is kind;
For his mercies aye endure,
Ever faithful, ever sure.

He, with all commanding might,
Filled the new-made world with light;
For his mercies aye endure,
Ever faithful, ever sure.

He the golden tressèd sun
Caused all day his course to run;
For his mercies aye endure,
Ever faithful, ever sure.

The hornèd moon to shine by night,
'Mid her spangled sisters bright;
For his mercies aye endure,
Ever faithful, ever sure.

All things living he doth feed;
His full hand supplies their need;
For his mercies aye endure,
Ever faithful, ever sure.

Let us with a gladsome mind
Praise the Lord, for he is kind;
For his mercies aye endure,
Ever faithful, ever sure.

John Milton

O LOVE THAT WILT NOT LET ME GO

O Love that wilt not let me go,
　　I rest my weary soul in Thee;
I give Thee back the life I owe,
That in Thine ocean depths its flow
　　May richer, fuller be.

O Light that followest all my way,
　　I yield my flickering torch to Thee;
My heart restores its borrowed ray,
That in Thy sunshine's blaze its day
　　May brighter, fairer be.

O Joy that seekest me through pain,
　　I cannot close my heart to Thee;
I trace the rainbow through the rain,
And feel the promise is not vain
　　That morn shall tearless be.

O Cross that liftest up my head,
　　I dare not ask to fly from Thee;
I lay in dust life's glory dead,
And from the ground there blossoms red
　　Life that shall endless be.

O Hope that lightenest all my way,
　　I cannot choose but cleave to Thee;
And wrestle till the break of day,
Disclose the wisdom of the way
　　In blessings yet to be.

George Matheson

4. The Word of the Lord

THE BARD

Hear the voice of the Bard,
Who present, past and future sees;
Whose ears have heard
The Holy Word
That walked among the ancient trees.

William Blake

THE WORD

O Earth! Thou hast not any wind that blows
Which is not music; every weed of thine
Pressed rightly flows in aromatic wine;
And humble hedge-row flower that grows,
And every little brown bird that doth sing,
Hath something greater than itself, and bears
A living word to every living thing,
Albeit holds the message unawares.
All shapes and sounds have something which is not
Of them: a spirit broods amid the grass;
Vague outlines of the Everlasting Thought
Lie in the melting shadows as they pass;
The touch of an eternal presence thrills
The fringes of the sunsets and the hills.

Richard Realf

O WORD OF GOD INCARNATE

O Word of God incarnate,
O Wisdom from on high,
O Truth unchanged, unchanging,
O Light of our dark sky,
We praise Thee for the radiance
That from the hallowed page,
A lantern to our footsteps,
Shines on from age to age.

The Church from her dear Master
Received the gift divine,
And still that light she lifteth
O'er all the earth to shine.
It is the golden casket,
Where gems of truth are stored;
It is the heaven-drawn picture
Of Christ, the living Word.

It floateth like a banner
Before God's host unfurled;
It shineth like a beacon
Above the darkling world;
It is the chart and compass
That o'er life's surging sea,
'Mid mists and rocks and quicksands,
Still guides, O Christ, to Thee.

O make Thy Church, dear Saviour,
A lamp of purest gold,
To bear before the nations
Thy true light, as of old.
O teach Thy wandering pilgrims
By this their path to trace,
Till, clouds and darkness ended,
They see Thee face to face.

William Walsham How

IN THE GARDEN OF THE LORD

The word of God came unto me,
Sitting alone among the multitudes;
And my blind eyes were touched with light.
And there was laid upon my lips a flame of fire.

I laugh and shout for life is good,
Though my feet are set in silent ways.
In merry mood I leave the crowd
To walk in my garden. Ever as I walk
I gather fruits and flowers in my hands.
And with joyful heart I bless the sun
That kindles all the place with radiant life.

I run with playful winds that blow the scent
Of rose and jasmine in eddying whirls.
At last I come where tall lilies grow,
Lifting their faces like white saints to God.
While the lilies pray, I kneel upon the ground;
I have strayed into the holy temple of the Lord.

Helen Keller

FROM THE LIGHT AND GLORY OF THE WORLD

The Spirit breathes upon the Word,
    And brings the truth to sight;
Precepts and promises afford
    A sanctifying sight.

A glory gilds the sacred page,
    Majestic like the sun;
It gives a light to ev'ry age,
    It gives, but borrows none.

William Cowper
45

FROM *BIBLIOLATRES*

God is not dumb, that he should speak no more;
    If thou hast wanderings in the wilderness
And findest not Sinai, 'tis thy soul is poor;
      There towers the mountain of the Voice no less,
Which whoso seeks shall find; but he who bends,
Intent on manna still and mortal ends,
      Sees it not, neither hears its thundered lore.

          James Russell Lowell

THE NINETEENTH PSALM

The heavens declare the glory of God;
    and the firmament sheweth his handywork.
Day unto day uttereth speech,
    and night unto night sheweth knowledge.
There is no speech nor language,
    where their voice is not heard.
Their line is gone out through all the earth,
    and their words to the end of the world.
In them hath he set a tabernacle for the sun,
    which is as a bridegroom coming out of his chamber,
      and rejoiceth as a strong man to run a race.
        His going forth is from the end of the heaven,
          and his circuit unto the ends of it:
            and there is nothing hid from the heat thereof.

The law of the Lord is perfect, converting the soul:
    the testimony of the Lord is sure, making wise the simple.
The statutes of the Lord are right, rejoicing the heart:
    the commandment of the Lord is pure, enlightening the eyes.
The fear of the Lord is clean, enduring for ever:
    the judgments of the Lord are true, and righteous altogether.
More to be desired are they than gold,
    yea, than much fine gold;
      sweeter also than honey and the honeycomb.

Moreover by them is thy servant warned:
  and in keeping of them there is great reward.
Who can understand his errors?
  cleanse thou me from secret faults.
Keep back thy servant also from presumptuous sins,
  let them not have dominion over me:
    then shall I be upright,
      and I shall be innocent
        from the great transgression.
Let the words of my mouth,
  and the meditation of my heart,
    be acceptable in thy sight, O Lord,
      my strength, and my redeemer.

THE BOOK

Softly I closed the Book as in a dream
And let its echoes linger to redeem
Silence with music, darkness with its gleam.

That day I worked no more. I could not bring
My hands to toil, my thoughts to trafficking.
A new light shone on every common thing.

Celestial glories flamed before my gaze.
That day I worked no more. But, to God's praise,
I shall work better all my other days.

Winfred Ernest Garrison

A BIT OF THE BOOK

A bit of the Book in the morning,
  To order my onward way.
A bit of the Book in the evening,
  To hallow the end of the day.

Margaret E. Sangster

THE BOOK OUR MOTHERS READ

We search the world for truth; we cull
The good, the pure, the beautiful,
From graven stone and written scroll,
And all old flower-fields of the soul;
And, weary seekers of the best,
We come back laden from the quest,
To find that all the sages said
Is in the Book our mothers read.

John Greenleaf Whittier

IN EARTHEN VESSELS

The dear Lord's best interpreters
    Are humble human souls;
The gospel of a life like His
    Is more than books or scrolls.

From scheme and creed the light goes out,
    The saintly fact survives;
The blessed Master none can doubt,
    Revealed in holy lives.

John Greenleaf Whittier

MORE TRUTH AND LIGHT

I am confident
        the Lord hath more truth
            and light
        yet to break forth
            out of His Word.

John Robinson (to the Pilgrims)

48

GOD'S WORD

I paused last eve beside the blacksmith's door,
  And heard the anvil ring, the vesper's chime,
And looking in I saw upon the floor
  Old hammers, worn with beating years of time.
"How many anvils have you had?" said I,
  "To wear and batter all these hammers so?"
"Just one," he answered. Then with twinkling eye:
  "The anvil wears the hammers out, you know."
And so, I thought, the anvil of God's Word
  For ages skeptics' blows have beat upon,
But though the noise of falling blows was heard
  The anvil is unchanged; the hammers gone.

John Clifford

THE SACRAMENT

He was the Word that spake it,
He took the bread and brake it;
And what that Word did make it,
I do believe and take it.

John Donne

THE BIBLE

Within this awful volume lies
The mystery of mysteries:
Happiest they of human race,
To whom their God has given grace
To read, to fear, to hope, to pray,
To lift the latch, to force the way;
But better had they ne'er been born,
Who read to doubt, or read to scorn.

Sir Walter Scott

THE WORLD'S BIBLE

Christ has no hands but our hands
    To do His work today;
He has no feet but our feet
    To lead men in His way;
He has no tongue but our tongues
    To tell men how He died;
He has no help but our help
    To bring them to His side.

We are the only Bible
    The careless world will read;
We are the sinner's gospel,
    We are the scoffer's creed;
We are the Lord's last message
    Given in deed and word—
What if the line is crooked?
    What if the type is blurred?

What if our hands are busy
    With other work than His?
What if our feet are walking
    Where sin's allurement is?
What if our tongues are speaking
    Of things His lips would spurn?
How can we hope to help Him
    Unless from Him we learn?

Annie Johnson Flint

OF THE INCOMPARABLE TREASURE
OF THE SCRIPTURES

Read not this Book, in any case,
    But with a single eye:
Read not, but first desire God's grace
    To understand thereby.

Author unknown

5. The Greatness and Glory of God

from *ENOCH ARDEN*

Cast all your cares on God; that anchor holds.
Is He not yonder in those uttermost
Parts of the morning? If I flee to these,
Can I go from Him? And the sea is His,
The sea is His; He made it.

Alfred Tennyson

THE ONE THOUSANDTH PSALM

O God, we thank Thee for everything.

For the sea and its waves, blue, green and gray and always wonderful;

For the beach and the breakers and the spray and the white foam on the rocks;

For the blue arch of heaven; for the clouds in the sky, white and gray and purple;

For the green of the grass; for the forests in their spring beauty; for the wheat and corn and rye and barley.

We thank Thee for all Thou hast made and that Thou hast called it good;

For all the glory and beauty and wonder of the world.

We thank Thee that Thou hast placed us in the world to subdue all things to Thy glory,

And to use all things for the good of Thy children.

Edward Everett Hale

HYMN OF JOY

Joyful, joyful, we adore Thee,
    God of glory, Lord of love;
Hearts unfold like flowers before Thee,
    Praising Thee their sun above.
Melt the clouds of sin and sadness;
    Drive the dark of doubt away;
Giver of immortal gladness,
    Fill us with the light of day!

All Thy works with joy surround Thee,
    Earth and heaven reflect Thy rays,
Stars and angels sing around Thee,
    Centre of unbroken praise:
Field and forest, vale and mountain,
    Blooming meadow, billowing sea,
Chanting bird and flowing fountain,
    Call us to rejoice in Thee.

Thou art giving and forgiving,
    Ever blessing, ever blest,
Well-spring of the joy of living,
    Ocean-depth of happy rest.
Thou our Father, Christ our Brother,—
    All who live in love are Thine:
Teach us how to love each other,
    Lift us to the Joy Divine.

Mortals join the mighty chorus,
    Which the morning stars began;
Father-love is reigning o'er us,
    Brother-love binds man to man.
Ever singing march we onward,
    Victors in the midst of strife;
Joyful music lifts us sunward
    In the triumph song of life.

Henry van Dyke

PIED BEAUTY

Glory be to God for dappled things—
    For skies of couple-colour as a brindled cow;
      For rose-moles all in stipple upon trout that swim;
Fresh-firecoal chestnut-falls; finches' wings;
    Landscape plotted and pieced—fold, fallow, and plough;
      And all trades, their gear and tackle and trim.

All things counter, original, spare, strange;
    Whatever is fickle, freckled (who knows how?)
      With swift, slow; sweet, sour; adazzle, dim;
He fathers-forth whose beauty is past change:
      Praise him.

Gerard Manley Hopkins

FROM *THE MARSHES OF GLYNN*

Ye marshes, how candid and simple and nothing-withholding
    and free
Ye publish yourselves to the sky and offer
    yourselves to the sea!
Tolerant plains, that suffer the sea and the rains and the sun,
Ye spread and span like the catholic man who hath mightily won
God out of knowledge and good out of infinite pain
And sight out of blindness and purity out of a stain.

As the marsh-hen secretly builds on the watery sod,
Behold I will build me a nest on the greatness of God:
I will fly in the greatness of God as the marsh-hen flies
In the freedom that fills all the space
    'twixt the marsh and the skies:
By so many roots as the marsh-grass sends in the sod
I will heartily lay me a-hold on the greatness of God:
Oh, like to the greatness of God is the greatness within
The range of the marshes, the liberal marshes of Glynn.

Sidney Lanier

53

GOD MAKES A PATH

God makes a path, provides a guide,
    And feeds a wilderness;
His glorious name, while breath remains,
    O that I may confess.

Lost many a time, I have had no guide,
    No house but a hollow tree!
In stormy winter night no fire,
    No food, no company;

In Him I found a house, a bed,
    A table, company;
No cup so bitter but's made sweet,
    Where God shall sweetening be.

Roger Williams

THANKSGIVING

Thank Thee, O Giver of Life, O God!
For the force that flames in the winter sod;
For the breath in my nostrils, fiercely good,
The sweet of water, the taste of food;
The sun that silvers the pantry floor,
The step of a neighbor at my door;
For dusk that fondles the window-pane,
For the beautiful sound of falling rain.

Thank Thee for love and light and air,
For children's faces, keenly fair,
For the wonderful joy of perfect rest
When the sun's wick lowers within the West;
For huddling hills in gowns of snow
Warming themselves in the afterglow;
For Thy mighty wings that are never furled,
Bearing onward the rushing world.

Thank Thee, O Giver of Life, O God!
For Thy glory leaping the lightning-rod;
For Thy terrible spaces of love and fire
Where sparks from the forge of Thy desire
Storm through the void in floods of suns,
Far as the heat of Thy Presence runs,
And where hurricanes of chanting spheres
Swing to the pulse of the flying years.

Thank Thee for human toil that thrills
With the plan of Thine which man fulfills;
For bridges and tunnels, for ships that soar,
For iron and steel and the furnace roar;
For this anguished vortex of blood and pain
Where sweat and struggle are never vain;
For progress, pushing the teeming earth
On and up to a higher birth.
Thank Thee for life, for life, for life,
O Giver of Life, O God!

Angela Morgan

IMMANENCE

Enthroned above the world although he sit,
Still in the world in him and he in it;
    The self-same power in yonder sunset glows
That kindled in the words of Holy Writ.

Richard Hovey

TRANSCENDENCE

Though one with all that sense or soul can see,
Not imprisoned in his own creations, he,
    His life is more than stars or winds or angels—
The sun doth not contain him nor the sea.

Richard Hovey

GOD THE ARCHITECT

Who Thou art I know not
   But this much I know:
Thou hast set the Pleiades
   In a silver row;

Thou hast sent the trackless winds
   Loose upon their way;
Thou hast reared a colored wall
   'Twixt the night and day;

Thou hast made the flowers to bloom
   And the stars to shine;
Hid rare gems of richest ore
   In the tunneled mine;

But chief of all Thy wondrous works
   Supreme of all Thy plan
Thou hast put an upward reach
   Into the heart of man.

Harry Kemp

BELIEF IN PLAN OF THEE

Whatever else withheld, withhold not from us,
Belief in plan of Thee enclosed in Time and Space;
Health, peace, salvation universal.

Is it a dream?
Nay, but the lack of it the dream,
And, failing it, love's lore and wealth a dream,
And all the world a dream.

Walt Whitman

I YIELD THEE PRAISE

For thoughts that curve like winging birds
Out of the summer dusk each time
I drink the splendor of the sky
And touch the wood-winds swinging by—
I yield Thee praise.

For waves that lift from autumn seas
To spill strange music on the land,
The broken nocturne of a lark
Flung out upon the lonely dark—
I yield Thee praise.

For rain that piles gray torrents down
Black mountain-gullies to the plain,
For singing fields and crimson flare
At daybreak, and the sea-sweet air—
I yield Thee praise.

For gentle mists that wander in
To hide the tired world outside
That in our hearts old lips may smile
Their blessing through life's afterwhile—
I yield Thee praise.

For hopes that fight like stubborn grass
Up through the clinging snows of fear
To find the rich earth richer still
With kindliness and honest will—
I yield Thee praise.

Philip Jerome Cleveland

THE LORD IS GOOD TO ALL

The Lord is good to all:
And his tender mercies are over all his works.

Psalm 145:9

GOD OF THE EARTH, THE SKY, THE SEA

God of the earth, the sky, the sea,
Maker of all above, below,
Creation lives and moves in Thee;
Thy present life through all doth flow.

Thy love is in the sun-shine's glow,
Thy life is in the quickening air;
When lightnings flash and storm winds blow,
There is Thy power, Thy law is there.

We feel Thy calm at evening's hour,
Thy grandeur in the march of night,
And when the morning breaks in power,
We hear Thy word, "Let there be light."

But higher far, and far more clear,
Thee in man's spirit we behold,
Thine image and Thyself are there,—
Th' in-dwelling God, proclaimed of old.

Samuel Longfellow

SILENCE

I need not shout my faith. Thrice eloquent
    Are quiet trees and the green listening sod;
Hushed are the stars, whose power is never spent;
    The hills are mute: yet how they speak of God!

Charles Hanson Towne

EACH IN HIS OWN TONGUE

A fire-mist and a planet—
    A crystal and a cell,
A jelly-fish and a saurian,
    And caves where the cave-men dwell;
Then a sense of law and beauty
    And a face turned from the clod,—
Some call it Evolution,
    And others call it God.

A haze on the far horizon,
    The infinite, tender sky,
The ripe, rich tint of the cornfields,
    And the wild geese sailing high;
And all over upland and lowland
    The charm of the golden-rod,—
Some of us call it Autumn,
    And others call it God.

Like tides on a crescent sea-beach,
    When the moon is new and thin,
Into our hearts high yearnings
    Come welling and surging in;
Come from the mystic ocean
    Whose rim no foot has trod,—
Some of us call it Longing
    And others call it God.

A picket frozen on duty,
    A mother starved for her brood,
Socrates drinking the hemlock,
    And Jesus on the rood;
And millions who, humble and nameless,
    The straight, hard pathway plod,—
Some call it Consecration,
    And others call it God.

                                William Herbert Carruth

FROM *SAMSON AGONISTES*

This only hope relieves me, that the strife
With me hath end; and the contest is now
'Twixt God and Dagon; Dagon hath presumed,
Me overthrown, to enter lists with God . . .
          . . . for God,
Nothing more certain, will not long defer
To vindicate the glory of his name
Against all competition, nor will long
Endure it, doubtful whether God be Lord,
Or Dagon.

John Milton

WHAT IS THE WORLD?

This is a piece too fair
To be the child of Chance, and not of Care.
No Atoms casually together hurl'd
Could e'er produce so beautiful a world.

John Dryden

MY MORNING SONG

O Lord of life, Thy quickening voice awakes my morning song!
In gladsome words I would rejoice that I to Thee belong.
I see Thy light, I feel Thy wind; the world, it is Thy word;
Whatever wakes my heart and mind Thy presence is, my Lord.
Therefore I choose my highest part, and turn my face to Thee;
Therefore I stir my inmost heart to worship fervently.

George Macdonald

II
MANKIND

6. *Desperation and Yearning*

EPITAPH, FOUND SOMEWHERE IN SPACE

In desolation, here a lost world lies.
All wisdom was its aim: with noble plan,
It sounded ocean deeps; measured the skies;
And fathomed every mystery but Man.

Hugh Wilgus Ramsaur

THE OLD STOIC

Riches I hold in light esteem,
    And Love I laugh to scorn;
And lust of fame was but a dream
    That vanish'd with the morn:

And, if I pray, the only prayer
    That moves my lips for me
Is, 'Leave the heart that now I bear,
    And give me liberty!'

Yea, as my swift days near their goal,
    'Tis all that I implore:
In life and death a chainless soul,
    With courage to endure.

Emily Brontë

ENOUGH NOT ONE

The poor have little,
Beggars none;
The rich too much,
Enough not one.

Benjamin Franklin

FROM ON THIS ISLAND

The judge enforcing the obsolete law,
The banker making the loan for the war,
The expert designing the long-range gun
To exterminate everyone under the sun,
Would like to get out but can only mutter;—
"What can I do? It's my bread and butter."

W. H. Auden

FROM SHINE, PERISHING REPUBLIC

And boys, be in nothing so moderate as in love of man,
a clever servant, insufferable master.
There is the trap that catches noblest spirits, that caught—
they say—God, when he walked on earth.

Robinson Jeffers

FROM MACBETH

Canst thou not minister to a mind diseas'd . . .
Cleanse the stuff'd bosom of that perilous stuff
Which weighs upon the heart?

William Shakespeare

FROM *IN MEMORY OF W. B. YEATS*

In the nightmare of the dark
All the dogs of Europe bark,
And the living nations wait,
Each sequestered in its hate;

Intellectual disgrace
Stares from every human face,
And the seas of pity lie
Locked and frozen in each eye.

W. H. Auden

ON SOME TREES NEEDLESSLY SLAIN

The woods shall not decry the murderous stroke
That shears the world's green living robe away,
Till, in a planet bare of pine and oak,
Deserts hold court on earth's last judgment day.

Stanton A. Coblentz

GOD

Day and night I wander widely
   through the wilderness of thought,
Catching dainty things of fancy most reluctant to be caught,
Shining tangles leading nowhere persistently unravel,
Tread strange paths of meditation very intricate to travel.

Gleaming bits of quaint desire tempt my steps
   beyond the decent,
I confound old solid glory with publicity too recent.
But my one unchanged obsession, wheresoe'er my feet have trod,
Is a keen, enormous, haunting, never-sated thirst for God.

Gamaliel Bradford

65

A LAST APPEAL

O somewhere, somewhere, God unknown,
    Exist and be!
I am dying; I am all alone;
    I must have Thee!
God! God! my sense, my soul, my all,
    Dies in the cry:—
Saw'st thou the faint star flame and fall?
    Ah! it was I.

                Frederick W. H. Myers

DOVER BEACH

The sea is calm to-night,
The tide is full, the moon lies fair
Upon the straits;—on the French coast the light
Gleams and is gone; the cliffs of England stand,
Glimmering and vast, out in the tranquil bay.
Come to the window, sweet is the night air!
Only, from the long line of spray
Where the sea meets the moon-blanch'd land,
Listen! you hear the grating roar
Of pebbles which the waves draw back, and fling,
At their return, up the high strand.
Begin, and cease, and then again begin,
With tremulous cadence slow, and bring
The eternal note of sadness in.

Sophocles long ago
Heard it on the Aegean, and it brought
Into his mind the turbid ebb and flow
Of human misery; we
Find also in the sound a thought,
Hearing it by this distant northern sea.

The Sea of Faith
Was once, too, at the full, and round earth's shore
Lay like the folds of a bright girdle furl'd.
But now I only hear
Its melancholy, long, withdrawing roar,
Retreating, to the breath
Of the night-wind, down the vast edges drear
And naked shingles of the world.
Ah, love, let us be true
To one another! for the world, which seems
To lie before us like a land of dreams,
So various, so beautiful, so new,
Hath really neither joy, nor love, nor light,
Nor certitude, nor peace, nor help for pain;
And we are here as on a darkling plain
Swept with confused alarms of struggle and flight,
Where ignorant armies clash by night.

Matthew Arnold

FROM *NIGHT*

Machinery is enough for a Scientist,
And Beauty is enough for a Poet;
But in the hearts of men and women, and in the thirsty hearts
    of little children
There is a hunger, and there is an unappeasable longing,
For a Father and for the love of a Father . . .
For the root of a soul is mystery,
And the Night is mystery,
And in that mystery men would open inward into Eternity,
And know love, the Lord.
Blessed be his works, and his angels, and his sons
    crowned with his glory!

James Oppenheim

67

THE MAN WITH THE HOE

*God made man in His own image
in the image of God made He him.*—GENESIS

Bowed by the weight of centuries he leans
Upon his hoe and gazes on the ground,
The emptiness of ages in his face,
And on his back the burden of the world.
Who made him dead to rapture and despair,
A thing that grieves not and that never hopes,
Stolid and stunned, a brother to the ox?
Who loosened and let down this brutal jaw?
Whose was the hand that slanted back this brow?
Whose breath blew out the light within this brain?

Is this the Thing the Lord God made and gave
To have dominion over sea and land;
To trace the stars and search the heavens for power;
To feel the passion of Eternity?
Is this the Dream He dreamed who shaped the suns
And pillared the blue firmament with light?
Down all the stretch of Hell to its last gulf
There is no shape more terrible than this—
More tongued with censure of the world's blind greed—
More filled with signs and portents for the soul—
More fraught with menace to the universe.

What gulfs between him and the seraphim!
Slave of the wheel of labor, what to him
Are Plato and the swing of Pleiades?
What the long reaches of the peaks of song,
The rift of dawn, the reddening of the rose?
Through this dread shape the suffering ages look;
Time's tragedy is in that aching stoop;
Through this dread shape humanity betrayed,
Plundered, profaned and disinherited,
Cries protest to the Judges of the World,
A protest that is also prophecy.

O masters, lords and rulers in all lands,
Is this the handiwork you give to God,
This monstrous thing distorted and soul-quenched?
How will you ever straighten up this shape;
Touch it again with immortality;
Give back the upward looking and the light;
Rebuild in it the music and the dream;
Make right the immemorial infamies,
Perfidious wrongs, immedicable woes?

O masters, lords and rulers in all lands,
How will the Future reckon with this Man?
How answer his brute question in that hour
When whirlwinds of rebellion shake the world?
How will it be with kingdoms and with kings—
With those who shaped him to the thing he is—
When this dumb Terror shall reply to God,
After the silence of the centuries?

Edwin Markham

THE JEW TO JESUS

O man of my own people, I alone
Among these alien ones can know thy face,
I who have felt the kinship of our race
Burn in me as I sit where they intone
Thy praises—those who, striving to make known
A God for sacrifice, have missed the grace
Of thy sweet human meaning in its place,
Thou who art of our blood-bond and our own.

Are we not sharers of thy Passion? Yea,
In spirit-anguish closely by thy side
We have drained the bitter cup, and, tortured, felt
With thee the bruising of each heavy welt.
In every land is our Gethsemane.
A thousand times have we been crucified.

Florence Kiper Frank

69

FROM *FOR THE TIME BEING*

Come to our well-run desert
Where anguish arrives by cable,
And the deadly sins
May be bought in tins
With instructions on the label.

W. H. Auden

THE DEBT

This is the debt I pay
Just for one riotous day,
Years of regret and grief,
Sorrow without relief.

Pay it I will to the end—
Until the grave, my friend,
Gives me a true release—
Gives me the clasp of peace.

Slight was the thing I bought,
Small was the debt I thought,
Poor was the loan at best—
God! but the interest!

Paul Laurence Dunbar

GUILTY

I never cut my neighbor's throat;
    My neighbor's gold I never stole;
I never spoiled his house and land;
    But God have mercy on my soul!

For I am haunted night and day
    By all the deeds I have not done;
O unattempted loveliness!
    O costly valor never won!

Marguerite Wilkinson

INDIFFERENCE

When Jesus came to Golgotha they hanged Him on a tree,
They drave great nails through hands and feet,
    and made a Calvary;
They crowned Him with a crown of thorns,
    red were His wounds and deep,
For those were crude and cruel days, the human flesh was cheap.

When Jesus came to Birmingham, they simply passed Him by,
They never hurt a hair of Him, they only let Him die;
For men had grown more tender, and they would not give Him pain,
They only just passed down the street, and left Him in the rain.

Still Jesus cried, "Forgive them,
    for they know not what they do,"
And still it rained the winter rain
    that drenched Him through and through;
The crowds went home and left the streets without a soul to see,
And Jesus crouched against a wall and cried for Calvary.

                    G. A. Studdert-Kennedy

EARTH'S NIGHT

    Earth's night is where she rolls
      In her own shade;
    And even thus the Soul's
      Dark hours are made.

                    William Allingham

VANITY OF VANITIES

Naked to earth was I brought—naked to earth I descend.
Why should I labour for nought, seeing how naked the end?

                Palladas (translated by William
                        M. Hardinge)

FROM *ESSAY ON MAN*

Know then thy selfe, presume not God to scan;
The proper study of Mankind is Man.
Plac'd on this isthmus of a middle state,
A Being darkly wise, and rudely great:
With too much knowledge for the Sceptic side,
With too much weakness for the Stoic's pride,
He hangs between; in doubt to act, or rest;
In doubt to deem himself a God, or Beast;
In doubt his Mind or Body to prefer;
Born but to die, and reas'ning but to err,
Alike in ignorance, his reason such,
Whether he thinks too little, or too much:
Chaos of Thought and Passion, all confus'd;
Still by himself abus'd, or disabus'd;
Created half to rise and half to fall;
Great lord of all things, yet a prey to all;
Sole judge of Truth, in endless Error hurl'd;
The glory, jest and riddle of the world.

Alexander Pope

CHORUS

Before the beginning of years
    There came to the making of man
Time, with a gift of tears;
    Grief, with a glass that ran;
Pleasure, with pain for leaven;
    Summer, with flowers that fell;
Remembrance fallen from heaven,
    And madness risen from hell;
Strength without hands to smite;
    Love that endures for a breath;
Night, the shadow of light,
    And life, the shadow of death.

And the high gods took in hand
    Fire, and the falling of tears,
And a measure of sliding sand
    From under the feet of the years;
And froth and drift of the sea;
    And dust of the labouring earth;
And bodies of things to be
    In the houses of death and of birth;
And wrought with weeping and laughter,
    And fashion'd with loathing and love,
With life before and after
    And death beneath and above,
For a day and a night and a morrow,
    That his strength might endure for a span
With travail and heavy sorrow,
    The holy spirit of man.

From the winds of the north and the south
    They gather'd as unto strife;
They breathed upon his mouth,
    They filled his body with life;
Eyesight and speech they wrought
    For the veils of the soul therein,
A time for labour and thought,
    A time to serve and to sin;
They gave him light in his ways,
    And love, and a space for delight,
And beauty and length of days,
    And night, and sleep in the night.
His speech is a burning fire;
    With his lips he travaileth;
In his heart is a blind desire,
    In his eyes foreknowledge of death;
He weaves, and is clothed with derision;
    Sows, and he shall not reap;
His life is a watch or a vision
    Between a sleep and a sleep.

Algernon Charles Swinburne

FROM *LEAVES OF GRASS*

I sit and look out upon all the sorrows of the world,
    and upon all oppression and shame;
I hear secret convulsive sobs from young men,
    at anguish with themselves, remorseful after deeds done;
I see, in low life, the mother misused by her children,
    dying, neglected, gaunt, desperate;
I see the wife misused by her husband—
    I see the treacherous seducer of young women;
I mark the ranklings of jealousy and unrequited love,
    attempted to be hid—I see these sights on the earth;
I see the workings of battle, pestilence, tyranny—
    I see martyrs and prisoners;
I observe a famine at sea—I observe the sailors
    casting lots who shall be kill'd,
    to preserve the lives of the rest;
I observe the slights and degradations
    cast by arrogant persons upon laborers, the poor,
    and upon negroes, and the like;
All these—all the meanness and agony without end,
    I sitting, look out upon,
See, hear, and am silent.

Walt Whitman

ON THE BIRTH OF HIS SON

Families, when a child is born
Want it to be intelligent.
I, through intelligence,
Having wrecked my whole life,
Only hope the baby will prove
Ignorant and stupid.
Then he will crown a tranquil life
By becoming a Cabinet Minister.

Su Tung-p'o (translated by Arthur Waley)

PAST AND PRESENT

I remember, I remember
The house where I was born,
The little window where the sun
Came peeping in at morn;
He never came a wink too soon
Nor brought too long a day;
But now, I often wish the night
Had borne my breath away.

I remember, I remember
The roses, red and white,
The violets, and the lily-cups—
Those flowers made of light!
The lilacs where the robin built,
And where my brother set
The laburnum on his birthday,—
The tree is living yet!

I remember, I remember
Where I was used to swing,
And thought the air must rush as fresh
To swallows on the wing;
My spirit flew in feathers then
That is so heavy now,
And summer pools could hardly cool
The fever on my brow.

I remember, I remember
The fir-trees dark and high;
I used to think their slender tops
Were close against the sky:
It was a childish ignorance,
But now 'tis little joy
To know I'm farther off from Heaven
Than when I was a boy.

Thomas Hood

FROM *MACBETH*

Tomorrow, and tomorrow, and tomorrow,
Creeps on this petty pace from day to day
To the last syllable of recorded time;
And all our yesterdays have lighted fools
The way to dusty death. Out, out, brief candle!
Life's but a walking shadow, a poor player
That struts and frets his hour upon the stage
And then is heard no more: it is a tale
Told by an idiot, full of sound and fury,
Signifying nothing.

William Shakespeare

FROM *ON THIS DAY I COMPLETE MY THIRTY-SIXTH YEAR*

My days are in the yellow leaf;
   The flowers and fruits of love are gone;
The worm, the canker, and the grief,
     Are mine alone!

The fire that in my bosom preys
   Is like to some volcanic isle;
No torch is kindled at its blaze,—
     A funeral pile.

The hope, the fear, the jealous care,
   The exalted portion of the pain
And power of love, I cannot share,
     But wear the chain.

George Gordon, Lord Byron

CALIBAN IN THE COAL MINES

God, we don't like to complain;
  We know that the mine is no lark.
But—there's the pools from the rain;
  But—there's the cold and the dark.

God, You don't know what it is—
  You, in Your well-lighted sky—
Watch the meteors whizz;
  Warm, with the sun always by.

God, if You had but the moon
  Stuck in Your cap for a lamp,
Even You'd tire of it soon,
  Down in the dark and the damp.

Nothing but blackness above
  And nothing that moves but the cars—
God, if You wish for our love,
  Fling us a handful of stars!

Louis Untermeyer

WRITTEN IN EARLY SPRING

I heard a thousand blended notes
While in a grove I sate reclined,
In that sweet mood when pleasant thoughts
Bring sad thoughts to the mind.

To her fair works did Nature link
The human soul that through me ran;
And much it grieved my heart to think
What man has made of man.

Through primrose tufts, in that sweet bower,
The periwinkle trail'd its wreaths;
And 'tis my faith that every flower
Enjoys the air it breathes.

77

The birds around me hopp'd and play'd,
Their thoughts I cannot measure,—
But the least motion which they made
It seem'd a thrill of pleasure.

The budding twigs spread out their fan
To catch the breezy air;
And I must think, do all I can,
That there was pleasure there.

If this belief from heaven be sent,
If such be Nature's holy plan,
Have I not reason to lament
What man has made of man?

William Wordsworth

FROM *THE RUBÁIYÁT OF OMAR KHAYYÁM*

For in and out, above, about, below,
'Tis nothing but a Magic Shadow-show,
    Play'd in a Box whose Candle is the Sun,
Round which we Phantom Figures come and go.

And if the Wine you drink, the Lip you press,
End in the Nothing all Things end in—Yes—
    Then fancy while Thou art, Thou art but what
Thou shalt be—Nothing—Thou shalt not be less.

While the Rose blows along the River Brink,
With old Khayyám the Ruby Vintage drink:
    And when the Angel with his darker Draught
Draws up to Thee—take that, and do not shrink.

'Tis all a Chequer-board of Nights and Days
Where Destiny with Men for Pieces plays:
    Hither and thither moves, and mates, and slays.
And one by one back in the Closet lays.

Edward FitzGerald

LIFE'S CHEQUER-BOARD

A Chequer-Board of mingled Light and Shade?
And We the Pieces on it deftly laid?
Moved and removed, without a word to say,
By the Same Hand that Board and Pieces made?

No pieces we in any Fateful Game,
Nor free to shift on Destiny the blame;
Each Soul doth tend its own immortal flame,
Fans it to Heaven, or smothers it in shame.

John Oxenham

THE NEWS

Companion Fear is at my side,
    I cannot make him leave,
He whispers horror in my ear,
    He twitches at my sleeve.

He presses down upon my heart,
    He catches at my breath,
He does not need to put in words
    The hovering of death.

Companion Fear is at my side,
    I cannot make him go,
For we are bound in common dread
    Of what we do not know.

Sec

ALL IS VANITY

I have seen all the works that are done under the sun;
    and, behold, all is vanity and vexation of spirit.
That which is crooked cannot be made straight:
    and that which is wanting cannot be numbered.
For that which befalleth the sons of men befalleth beasts;
    even one thing befalleth them:
        as the one dieth, so dieth the other;
    yea, they have all one breath;
        so that a man hath no preëminence above a beast:
        for all is vanity.

Ecclesiastes 1:14-15; 3:19

FROM *IN MEMORIAM*

Our little systems have their day;
    They have their day and cease to be;
    They are but broken lights of thee,
And thou, O Lord, art more than they.

We have but faith: we cannot know;
    For knowledge is of things we see;
    And yet we trust it comes from thee,
A beam in darkness: let it grow.

Let knowledge grow from more to more,
    But more of reverence in us dwell;
    That mind and soul, according well,
May make one music as before.

But vaster. We are fools and slight;
    We mock thee when we do not fear;
    But help thy foolish ones to hear;
Help thy vain worlds to bear thy light.

Alfred Tennyson

7.   Remorse and Repentance

I SAW GOD WASH THE WORLD

I saw God wash the world last night
　With His sweet showers on high,
And then, when morning came, I saw
　Him hang it out to dry.

He washed each tiny blade of grass
　And every trembling tree;
He flung His showers against the hill,
　And swept the billowing sea.

The white rose is a cleaner white,
　The red rose is more red,
Since God washed every fragrant face
　And put them all to bed.

There's not a bird, there's not a bee
　That wings along the way
But is a cleaner bird and bee
　Than it was yesterday.

I saw God wash the world last night.
　Ah, would He had washed me
As clean of all my dust and dirt
　As that old white birch tree.

William L. Stidger

THE LOOK

The Saviour looked on Peter. Ay, no word,
No gesture of reproach; the Heavens serene
Though heavy with armed justice, did not lean
Their thunders that way: the forsaken Lord
Looked only, on the traitor. None record
What that look was, none guess; for those who have seen
Wronged lovers loving through a death-pang keen,
Or pale-cheeked martyrs smiling to a sword,
Have missed Jehovah at the judgment-call.
And Peter, from the height of blasphemy—
"I never knew this man"—did quail and fall
As knowing straight *that God*; and turnèd free
And went out speechless from the face of all,
And filled the silence, weeping bitterly.

Elizabeth Barrett Browning

THE MEANING OF THE LOOK

I think that look of Christ might seem to say—
"Thou Peter! art thou then a common stone
Which I at last must break my heart upon,
For all God's charge to his high angels may
Guard my foot better? Did I yesterday
Wash *thy* feet, my beloved, that they should run
Quick to deny me 'neath the morning sun?
And do thy kisses, like the rest, betray?
The cock crows coldly.—Go, and manifest
A late contrition, but no bootless fear!
For when thy final need is dreariest,
Thou shalt not be denied, as I am here;
My voice to God and angels shall attest,
Because I know this man, let him be clear."

Elizabeth Barrett Browning

A LAST PRAYER

Father, I scarcely dare to pray,
  So clear I see, now it is done,
That I have wasted half my day,
  And left my work but just begun;

So clear I see that things I thought
  Were right or harmless were a sin;
So clear I see that I have sought
  Unconscious, selfish aims to win;

So clear I see that I have hurt
  The soul I might have helped to save;
That I have slothful been, inert,
  Deaf to the calls thy leaders gave.

In outskirts of thy kingdom vast,
  Father, the humblest spot give me;
Set me the lowliest task thou hast,
  Let me repentant work for thee.

Helen Hunt Jackson

THE DOOMED MAN

There is a time, we know not when,
  A point we know not where,
That marks the destiny of men,
  For glory or despair.

There is a line, by us unseen,
  That crosses every path;
The hidden boundary between
  God's patience and His wrath.

Joseph Addison Alexander

83

THE GIFTS OF GOD

When God at first made Man,
Having a glass of blessing standing by;
Let us (said He) pour on him all we can:
Let the world's riches, which dispersèd lie,
    Contract into a span.

So strength first made a way;
Then beauty flow'd, then wisdom, honour, pleasure:
When almost all was out, God made a stay,
Perceiving that alone, of all His treasure,
    Rest in the bottom lay.

For if I should (said He)
Bestow this jewel also on my creature,
He would adore my gifts instead of me,
And rest in Nature, not the God of Nature:
    So both should losers be.

Yet let him keep the rest;
But keep them with repining restlessness:
Let him be rich and weary, that at least,
If goodness lead him not, yet weariness
    May toss him to my breast.

George Herbert

THE BATTLE WITHIN

God strengthen me to bear myself;
That heaviest weight of all to bear,
Inalienable weight of care.

All others are outside myself;
I lock my door and bar them out,
The turmoil, tedium, gad-about.

I lock my door upon myself,
And bar them out; but who shall wall
Self from myself, most loathed of all?

If I could once lay down myself,
And start self-purged upon the race
That all must run! Death runs apace.

If I could set aside myself,
And start with lightened heart upon
The road by all men overgone!

God harden me against myself,
This coward with pathetic voice
Who craves for ease, and rest, and joys:

Myself, arch-traitor to myself;
My hollowest friend, my deadliest foe,
My clog whatever road I go.

Yet One there is can curb myself,
Can roll the strangling load from me,
Break off the yoke and set me free.

Christina Rossetti

L'ENVOI

O Love triumphant over guilt and sin,
My soul is soiled, but Thou shalt enter in;
My feet must stumble if I walk alone,
Lonely my heart till beating by Thine own;
My will is weakness till it rest in Thine,
Cut off, I wither, thirsting for the Vine;
My deeds are dry leaves on a sapless tree,
My life is lifeless till it live in Thee!

Frederic L. Knowles

HIS PRAYER FOR ABSOLUTION

For those my unbaptized rhymes,
Writ in my wild unhallowed times;
For every sentence, clause and word,
That's not inlaid with Thee (my Lord),
Forgive me, God, and blot each line
Out of my book, that is not Thine.
But if, 'mongst all, Thou find'st here one
Worthy Thy benediction;
That one of all the rest, shall be
The glory of my work, and me.

Robert Herrick

THE SIN OF OMISSION

It isn't the thing you do;
    It's the thing you leave undone,
Which gives you a bit of heartache
    At the setting of the sun.

The tender word forgotten,
    The letter you did not write,
The flower you might have sent,
    Are your haunting ghosts at night.

The stone you might have lifted
    Out of a brother's way,
The bit of heartsome counsel
    You were hurried too much to say;

The loving touch of the hand,
    The gentle and winsome tone,
That you had no time or thought for
    With troubles enough of your own.

The little acts of kindness,
　So easily out of mind;
Those chances to be helpful
　Which everyone may find—

No, it's not the thing you do,
　It's the thing you leave undone,
Which gives you the bit of heartache
　At the setting of the sun.

Margaret E. Sangster

SOMETIMES

Across the fields of yesterday
　He sometimes comes to me,
A little lad just back from play—
　The lad I used to be.

And yet he smiles so wistfully
　Once he has crept within,
I wonder if he hopes to see
　The man I might have been.

Thomas S. Jones, Jr.

THE TOUCH OF THE MASTER'S HAND

'Twas battered and scarred, and the auctioneer
Thought it scarcely worth his while
To waste much time on the old violin,
But held it up with a smile.
"What am I bidden, good folks," he cried,
"Who will start bidding for me?
A dollar, a dollar"—then, "Two!" "Only two?
Two dollars, and who'll make it three?

Three dollars once; three dollars, twice;
Going for three—" But no,
From the room, far back, a gray-haired man
Came forward and picked up the bow;
Then, wiping the dust from the old violin,
And tightening the loose strings,
He played a melody pure and sweet
As sweet as a caroling angel sings.

The music ceased, and the auctioneer,
With a voice that was quiet and low,
Said, "What am I bidden for the old violin?
And he held it up with the bow.
"A thousand dollars, and who'll make it two?
Two thousand! And who'll make it three?
Three thousand, once; three thousand, twice;
And going, and gone!" said he.
The people cheered, but some of them cried,
"We do not quite understand
What changed its worth?" Swift came the reply:
"The touch of the master's hand."

And many a man with life out of tune,
And battered and scattered with sin,
Is auctioned cheap to the thoughtless crowd,
Much like the old violin.
A "mess of pottage," a glass of wine;
A game—and he travels on.
He's "going" once, and "going" twice,
He's "going" and "almost gone."
But the Master comes, and the foolish crowd
Never can quite understand
The worth of a soul, and the change that's wrought
By the touch of the Master's hand.

Myra Brooks Welch

THE HOUND OF HEAVEN

I fled Him, down the nights and down the days;
    I fled Him, down the arches of the years;
I fled Him, down the labyrinthine ways
    Of my own mind; and in the mist of tears
I hid from Him, and under running laughter.
        Up vistaed hopes, I sped;
        And shot, precipitated,
Adown Titanic glooms of chasmed fears,
    From those strong Feet that followed, followed after.
        But with unhurrying chase,
        And unperturbed pace,
    Deliberate speed, majestic instancy,
        They beat—and a Voice beat
        More instant than the Feet—
    'All things betray thee, who betrayest Me.'

        I pleaded, outlaw-wise,
By many a hearted casement, curtained red,
    Trellised with intertwining charities;
(For, though I knew His love Who followèd,
        Yet was I sore adread
Lest, having Him, I must have naught beside.)
But, if one little casement parted wide,
    The gust of His approach would clash it to.
    Fear wist not to evade as Love wist to pursue.
Across the margent of the world I fled,
    And troubled the gold gateways of the stars,
    Smiting for shelter on their clangèd bars;
        Fretted to dulcet jars
And silvern chatter the pale ports o' the moon.
I said to dawn: Be sudden; to eve: Be soon—
    With thy young skyey blossoms heap me over
        From this tremendous Lover!
Float thy vague veil about me, lest He see!
    I tempted all His servitors, but to find

My own betrayal in their constancy,
In faith to Him their fickleness to me,
   Their traitorous trueness, and their loyal deceit.
To all swift things for swiftness did I sue;
    Clung to the whistling mane of every wind.
        But whether they swept, smoothly fleet,
     The long savannahs of the blue;
       Or whether, Thunder-driven,
      They clanged His chariot 'thwart a heaven,
Plashy with flying lightnings round the spurn o' their feet:—
   Fear wist not to evade as Love wist to pursue.
       Still with unhurrying chase,
       And unperturbèd pace,
   Deliberate speed, majestic instancy,
      Came on the following Feet,
      And a Voice above their beat—
'Naught shelters thee, who wilt not shelter Me.'

I sought no more that after which I strayed
     In face of man or maid;
But still within the little children's eyes
    Seems something, something that replies,
They at least are for me, surely for me!
I turned me to them very wistfully;
But just as their young eyes grew sudden fair
    With dawning answers there,
Their angel plucked them from me by the hair.
'Come then, ye other children, Nature's—share
With me' (said I) 'your delicate fellowship;
    Let me greet you lip to lip,
    Let me twine with you caresses,
      Wantoning
    With our Lady-Mother's vagrant tresses.
      Banqueting
    With her in her wind-walled palace,
    Underneath her azured dais,
    Quaffing, as your taintless way is,
      From a chalice
Lucent-weeping out of the dayspring.'

So it was done:
I in their delicate fellowship was one—
Drew the bolt of Nature's secrecies;
I knew all the swift importings
On the wilful face of skies;
I knew how the clouds arise,
Spumèd of the wild sea-snortings;
All that's born or dies
Rose and drooped with; made them shapers
Of mine own moods, or wailful or divine—
With them joyed and was bereaven.
I was heavy with the even,
When she lit her glimmering tapers
Round the day's dead sanctities.
I laughed in the morning's eyes.
I triumphed and I saddened with all weather,
Heaven and I wept together,
And its sweet tears were salt with mortal mine;
Against the red throb of its sunset-heart
I laid my own to beat
And share commingling heat;
But not by that, by that, was eased my human smart.
In vain my tears were wet on Heaven's gray cheek.
For ah! we know not what each other says,
These things and I; in sound I speak—
Their sound is but their stir, they speak by silences.
Nature, poor stepdame, cannot slake my drouth;
Let her, if she would owe me,
Drop yon blue bosom-veil of sky, and show me
The breasts o' her tenderness:
Never did any milk of hers once bless
My thirsting mouth.
Nigh and nigh draws the chase,
With unperturbèd pace,
Deliberate speed, majestic instancy,
And past those noisèd Feet
A Voice comes yet more fleet—
'Lo! naught contents thee, who content'st not Me.'

Naked I wait Thy love's uplifted stroke!
My harness piece by piece Thou hast hewn from me,
      And smitten me to my knee;
      I am defenseless utterly.
      I slept, methinks, and woke,
And, slowly gazing, find me stripped in sleep.
In the rash lustihead of my young powers,
      I shook the pillaring hours
And pulled my life upon me; grimed with smears,
I stand amid the dust o' the mounded years—
My mangled youth lies dead beneath the heap.
My days have crackled and gone up in smoke,
Have puffed and burst as sun-starts on a stream.
      Yea, faileth now even dream
The dreamer, and the lute the lutanist;
Even the linkèd fantasies, in whose blossomy twist
I swung the earth a trinket at my wrist,
Are yielding; cords of all too weak account
For earth, with heavy griefs so overplussed,
      Ah! is Thy love indeed
A weed, albeit an amaranthine weed,
Suffering no flowers except its own to mount?
      Ah! must—
      Designer infinite!—
Ah! must Thou char the wood ere Thou canst limn with it?
My freshness spent its wavering shower i' the dust;
And now my heart is as a broken fount,
Wherein tear-dripping stagnate, split down ever
     From the dank thoughts that shiver
Upon the sightful branches of my mind.
     Such is; what is to be?
The pulp so bitter, how shall taste the rind?
I dimly guess what Time in mists confounds;
Yet ever and anon a trumpet sounds
From the hid battlements of Eternity:
Those shaken mists a space unsettle, then
Round the half-glimpsèd turrets slowly wash again;
     But not ere him who summoneth

I first have seen, enwound
With glooming robes purpureal, cypress-crowned;
His name I know, and what his trumpet saith.
Whether man's heart or life it be which yields
    Thee harvest, must Thy harvest fields
    Be dunged with rotten death?

    Now of that long pursuit
    Comes on at hand the bruit;
That Voice is round me like a bursting sea:
    'And is thy earth so marred,
    Shattered in shard on shard?
Lo, all things fly thee, for thou fliest Me!
    Strange, piteous, futile thing!
Wherefore should any set thee love apart?
Seeing none but I makes much of naught'
    (He said),
'And human love needs human meriting:
    How hast thou merited—.
Of all man's clotted clay the dingiest clot?
    Alack, thou knowest not
How little worthy of any love thou art!
Whom wilt thou find to love ignoble thee,
    Save Me, save only Me?
All which I took from thee I did but take,
    Not for thy harms,
But just that thou might'st seek it in My arms,
    All which thy child's mistake
Fancies as lost, I have stored for thee at home:
    Rise, clasp My hand, and come!'
    Halts by me that footfall:
    Is my gloom, after all,
Shade of His hand, outstretched caressingly?
    'Ah, fondest, blindest, weakest,
    I am He Whom thou seekest!
Thou dravest love from thee, who dravest Me.'

Francis Thompson

8. Challenge and Decision

GET SOMEBODY ELSE

The Lord had a job for me,
  But I had so much to do,
I said, "You get somebody else,
  Or wait till I get through."
I don't know how the Lord came out,
  But He seemed to get along,
But I felt kind o' sneakin' like—
  Knowed I'd done God wrong.

One day I needed the Lord—
  Needed Him right away;
But He never answered me at all,
  And I could hear Him say,
Down in my accusin' heart:
  "Nigger, I'se got too much to do;
You get somebody else,
  Or wait till I get through."

Now, when the Lord He have a job for me,
  I never tries to shirk;
I drops what I has on hand,
  And does the good Lord's work.
And my affairs can run along,
  Or wait till I get through;
Nobody else can do the work
  That God marked out for you.

Paul Laurence Dunbar

FROM *SAINT PAUL*

Whoso has felt the Spirit of the Highest
   Cannot confound nor doubt Him nor deny:
Yea, with one voice, O world, tho' thou deniest,
   Stand thou on that side, for on this am I.

Frederic W. H. Myers

LIFE

Forenoon and afternoon and night,—
   Forenoon
And afternoon, and night,—Forenoon, and—
   what!
The empty song repeats itself. No more?
Yea, that is Life: make this forenoon sublime,
This afternoon a psalm, this night a prayer,
And Time is conquered, and thy crown is won.

Edward Rowland Sill

BE TRUE

Thou must be true thyself
   If thou the truth wouldst teach;
Thy soul must overflow if thou
   Another's soul wouldst reach!
It needs the overflow of heart
   To give the lips full speech.

Think truly, and thy thoughts
   Shall the world's famine feed;
Speak truly, and each word of thine
   Shall be a fruitful seed;
Live truly, and thy life shall be
   A great and noble creed.

Horatius Bonar

HE DOETH ALL THINGS WELL

I hoped that with the brave and strong,
My portioned task might lie;
To toil amid the busy throng,
With purpose pure and high;
But God has fixed another part,
And He has fixed it well,
I said so with my breaking heart,
When first this trouble fell.

These weary hours will not be lost,
These days of misery,
These nights of darkness, anguish-tossed,
Can I but turn to Thee:
With secret labour to sustain
In patience every blow
To gather fortitude from pain,
And holiness from woe.

If Thou shouldst bring me back to life,
More humble I should be,
More wise, more strengthened for the strife,
More apt to lean on Thee;
Should death be standing at the gate,
Thus should I keep my vow;
But, Lord, whatever be my fate,
O let me serve Thee now!

Anne Brontë

FROM *HAMLET*

This above all: to thine own self be true,
And it must follow, as the night the day,
Thou canst not then be false to any man.

William Shakespeare

THE LAST DEFILE

He died climbing.—A SWISS GUIDE'S EPITAPH

Make us Thy mountaineers:
We would not linger on the lower slope,
Fill us afresh with hope, O God of Hope,
That undefeated we may climb the hill
As seeing Him who is invisible.

Let us die climbing. When this little while
Lies far behind us, and the last defile
Is all alight, and in that light we see
Our Leader and our Lord, what will it be?

Amy Carmichael

FROM *PROLOGUE* OF *FAUST*

Lose this day loitering, 'twill be the same story
Tomorrow, and the next more dilatory;
Each indecision brings its own delays,
And days are lost lamenting o'er lost days.
Are you in earnest? Seize this very minute!
Boldness has genius, power, and magic in it.
Only engage, and then the mind grows heated.
Begin, and then the work will be completed.

John Anster

JUDGMENT DAY

Every day is Judgment Day,
Count on no to-morrow.
He who will not, when he may,
Act to-day, to-day, to-day,
Doth but borrow
Sorrow.

John Oxenham

I BIND MY HEART

I bind my heart this tide
To the Galilean's side,
To the wounds of Calvary—
To the Christ who died for me.

I bind my soul this day
To the brother far away,
To the brother near at hand,
In this town, and in this land.

I bind my heart in thrall
To the God, the Lord of all,
To the God, the poor man's Friend,
And the Christ whom He didst send.

I bind myself to peace,
To make strife and envy cease,
God! knit Thou sure the cord
Of my thralldom to my Lord.

Lauchlan MacLean Watt

THE WAYS

To every man there openeth
A Way, and Ways, and a Way.
And the High Soul climbs the High Way,
And the Low Soul gropes the Low,
And in between, on the misty flats,
The rest drift to and fro.
But to every man there openeth
A High Way, and a Low.
And every man decideth
The Way his soul shall go.

John Oxenham

FROM THE GATE OF THE YEAR

And I said to the man who stood at the gate of the year:
"Give me a light, that I may tread safely into the unknown!"
And he replied:
'Go out into the darkness and put your hand into the Hand of God.
That shall be to you better than light and safer than a known way."
So, I went forth, and finding the Hand of God, trod gladly into
    the night.
And He led me toward the hills and the breaking of day in the
    lone East.

M. Louise Haskins

THE MIDDLE-TIME

Between the exhilaration of Beginning . . .
    And the satisfaction of Concluding,
      Is the Middle-Time
        of Enduring . . . Changing . . . Trying . . .
          Despairing . . . Continuing . . . Becoming.

Jesus Christ was the Man of God's Middle-Time
    Between Creation and . . . Accomplishment.
Through him God said of Creation,
    "Without mistake."
And of Accomplishment,
    "Without doubt."

And we in our Middle-Times
    of Wondering and Waiting,
      Hurrying and Hesitating,
      Regretting and Revising—
We who have begun many things . . .
    and seen but few completed—
We who are becoming more . . . and less—
Through the evidence of God's Middle-Time

Have a stabilizing hint
    That we are not mistakes,
    That we are irreplaceable,
    That our Being is of interest,
       and our Doing is of purpose,
    That our Being and our Doing
       are surrounded by *Amen.*

Jesus Christ is the Completer
    of unfinished people
    with unfinished work
    in unfinished times.

May he keep us from sinking, from ceasing,
    from wasting, from solidifying,
That we may be for him
    Experimenters, Enablers, Encouragers,
    and Associates in Accomplishment.

                    Lona M. Fowler

FROM *BISHOP BLOUGRAM'S APOLOGY*

When the fight begins within himself,
A man's worth something. God stoops o'er his head,
Satan looks up between his feet,—both tug—
He's left, himself, i' the middle: the Soul wakes
And grows. Prolong that battle through his life!
Never leave growing till the life to come!

                    Robert Browning

QUO VADIS?

Fare not abroad, O Soul, to win
    Man's friendly smile or favoring nod;
Be still, be strong, and seek within
    The Comradeship of God.

> Beyond lies not the journey's end;
>   The fool goes wayfaring apart,
> And even as he goes his Friend
>   Is knocking at his heart.

Myles Connolly

THEY THAT WAIT UPON THE LORD

Hast thou not known?
Hast thou not heard,
    that the everlasting God,
        the Lord
            the Creator of the ends of the earth,
                fainteth not,
                    neither is weary?
there is no searching of His understanding.

He giveth power to the faint,
    and to them that have no might
        He increaseth strength.

Even the youths shall faint
    and be weary,
        and the young men shall utterly fall.

But they that wait upon the Lord
    shall renew their strength:
        they shall mount up with wings as eagles,
            they shall run and not be weary,
                and they shall walk,
                    and not faint.

Isaiah the Prophet (Isaiah 40:28-31)

101

9. Quest and Adventure

HE WHOM A DREAM HATH POSSESSED

He whom a dream hath possessed knoweth no more of doubting,
For mist and the blowing of winds and the mouthing of words he
    scorns;
Not the sinuous speech of schools he hears,
    but a knightly shouting,
And never comes darkness down, yet he greeteth a million morns.

He who a dream hath possessed knoweth no more of roaming;
All roads and the flowing of waves and the speediest flight he
    knows,
But wherever his feet are set, his soul is forever homing,
And going, he comes, and coming he heareth a call and goes.

He whom a dream hath possessed knoweth no more of sorrow,
At death and the dropping of leaves and the fading
    of suns he smiles,
For a dream remembers no past, and scorns the desire of a morrow,
And a dream in a sea of doom sets surely the ultimate isles.

He whom a dream hath possessed treads the impalpable marches,
From the dust of the day's long road he leaps to a
    laughing star,
And the ruin of worlds that fall he views from eternal arches,
And rides God's battlefield in a flashing and golden car.

Shaemas O'Sheel

PRAYER

Lord, the newness of this day
Calls me to an untried way:
Let me gladly take the road,
Give me strength to bear my load,
Thou my guide and helper be—
I will travel through with Thee.

Henry van Dyke

BUILDERS

We would be building; temples still undone
  O'er crumbling walls their crosses scarcely lift
Waiting till love can raise the broken stone,
  And hearts creative bridge the human rift;
We would be building, Master, let Thy plan
  Reveal the life that God would give to man.

Teach us to build; upon the solid rock
  We set the dream that hardens into deed,
Ribbed with the steel that time and change doth mock,
  Th' unfailing purpose of our noblest creed;
Teach us to build; O Master, lend us sight
  To see the towers gleaming in the light.

O keep us building, Master; may our hands
  Ne'er falter when the dream is in our hearts,
When to our ears there come divine commands
  And all the pride of sinful will departs;
We build with Thee, O grant enduring worth
  Until the heav'nly Kingdom comes on earth.

Purd E. Deitz

EARTH IS ENOUGH

We men of Earth have here the stuff
Of Paradise—we have enough!
We need no other stones to build
The Temple of the Unfulfilled—
No other ivory for the doors—
No other marble for the floors—
No other cedar for the beam
And dome of man's immortal dream.

Here on the paths of every-day—
Here on the common human way
Is all the stuff the gods would take
To build a Heaven, to mold and make
New Edens. Ours the stuff sublime
To build Eternity in time!

Edwin Markham

VICTORIA

Be of good cheer, I have overcome the world.—JOHN 16:33

Thy victory is in the heart,
    Thy kingdom is within;
When outward pride and pomp depart,
    Thy glory doth begin.

Thine army, ever in the field,
    Is led by love and light;
Thy followers fall but never yield,
    Triumphant in the right.

O King most meek and wonderful,
    Grant us among Thy host,
To follow Thee, to fight for Thee,
    Knights of the Holy Ghost.

Henry van Dyke

FROM *GUINEVERE*

I made them lay their hands in mine and swear
To reverence the King, as if he were
Their conscience, and their conscience as their King,
To break the heathen and uphold the Christ,
To ride abroad redressing human wrongs,
To speak no slander, no, nor listen to it.
To honor his own word as if his God's,
To lead sweet lives of purest chastity,
To love one maiden only, cleave to her,
And worship her by years of noble deeds,
Until they won her; for indeed I knew
Of no more subtle master under heaven
Than is the maiden passion for a maid,
Not only to keep down the base in man,
But teach high thought, and amiable words
And courtliness, and the desire of fame,
And love of truth, and all that makes a man.

Alfred Tennyson

FROM *ULYSSES*

I am a part of all that I have met;
Yet all experience is an arch wherethro'
Gleams that untravell'd world whose margin fades
For ever and for ever when I move.
How dull it is to pause, to make an end,
To rust unburnish'd, not to shine in use!
As tho' to breathe were life! Life piled on life
Were all too little, and of one to me
Little remains; but every hour is saved
From that eternal silence, something more,
A bringer of new things; and vile it were
For some three suns to store and hoard myself,
And this gray spirit yearning in desire

To follow knowledge like a sinking star,
Beyond the utmost bound of human thought.

Alfred Tennyson

FROM *THE PASSAGE TO INDIA*

Sail forth—steer for the deep waters only,
Reckless, O soul, exploring, I with thee and thou with me,
For we are bound where mariner has not yet dared to go,
And we will risk the ship, ourselves and all.

O my brave soul!
O farther, farther sail!
O daring joy, but safe! Are they not all the seas of God?
O farther, farther, farther sail!

Walt Whitman

FROM *THE PRESENT CRISIS*

Once to every man and nation comes the moment to decide,
In the strife of Truth with Falsehood, for the good
    or evil side;
Some great cause, God's new Messiah, offering each
    the bloom or blight,
Parts the goats upon the left hand, and the sheep
    upon the right,
And the choice goes by forever 'twixt that darkness
    and that light.

*   *   *

New occasions teach new duties; Time makes ancient good
    uncouth;
They must upward still, and onward, who would keep
    abreast of Truth;
Lo, before us gleam her camp-fires! we ourselves
    must Pilgrims be,

Launch our Mayflower, and steer boldly through
    the desperate winter sea,
Nor attempt the Future's portal with the Past's
    blood-rusted key.

James Russell Lowell

FROM *PRAYER OF COLUMBUS*

All my emprises have been fill'd with Thee,
My speculations, plans, begun and carried on
    in thoughts of Thee,
Sailing the deep or journeying the land for Thee;
Intentions, purports, aspirations mine,
    leaving results to Thee.

       *   *   *

One effort more, my altar this bleak sand;
That Thou O God my life hast lighted,
With ray of light, steady, ineffable, vouchsafed of Thee,
Light rare untellable, lighting the very light,
Beyond all signs, descriptions, languages;
For that O God, be it my latest word, here on my knees,
Old, poor, and paralyzed, I thank Thee.

My terminus near,
The clouds already closing in upon me,
The voyage balk'd, the course disputed, lost,
I yield my ships to Thee.

Walt Whitman

IN SPITE OF SORROW

In spite of sorrow, loss, and pain,
    Our course be onward still;
We sow on Burmah's barren plain,
    We reap on Zion's hill.

Adoniram Judson

107

AWAKE, AWAKE TO LOVE AND WORK

Awake, awake to love and work!
The lark is in the sky;
The fields are wet with diamond dew;
The worlds awake to cry
Their blessings on the Lord of life,
As he goes meekly by.

Come, let thy voice be one with theirs,
Shout with their shout of praise;
See how the giant sun soars up,
Great Lord of years and days!
So let the love of Jesus come
And set thy soul ablaze.

To give and give, and give again,
What God hath given thee;
To spend thyself nor count the cost;
To serve right gloriously
The God who gave all worlds that are,
And all that are to be.

G. A. Studdert-Kennedy

FROM *STOPPING BY WOODS ON A SNOWY EVENING*

The woods are lovely, dark and deep,
But I have promises to keep,
And miles to go before I sleep,
And miles to go before I sleep.

Robert Frost

These lines have been among the favorite quotations of Dr. Thomas Dooley and of President John F. Kennedy.

108

FROM *RHYMES OF A ROLLING STONE*

Thank God! there is always a Land of Beyond
　　For us who are true to the trail;
A vision to seek, a beckoning peak,
　　A farness that never will fail;
A pride in our soul that mocks at a goal,
　　A manhood that irks at a bond,
And try how we will, unattainable still,
　　Behold it, our Land of Beyond!

Robert W. Service

WIND AND LYRE

Thou art the wind and I the lyre:
　　Strike, O Wind, on the sleeping strings—
　　Strike till the dead heart stirs and sings!
I am the altar and thou the fire:
　　Burn, O Fire, to a snowy flame—
　　Burn me clean of the mortal blame!

I am the night and thou the dream:
　　Touch me softly and thrill me deep,
　　When all is white on the hills of sleep.
Thou art the moon and I the stream:
　　Shine to the trembling heart of me,
　　Light my soul to the mother-sea.

Edwin Markham

A PRAYER

God, give me sympathy and sense,
　　And help me keep my courage high;
God, give me calm and confidence,
　　And—please—a twinkle in my eye. Amen.

Margaret Bailey

TO-DAY

To be alive in such an age!
With every year a lightning page
Turned in the world's great wonder book
Whereon the leaning nations look.
When men speak strong for brotherhood,
For peace and universal good,
When miracles are everywhere,
And every inch of common air
Throbs a tremendous prophecy
Of greater marvels yet to be.
    O thrilling age,
    O willing age!
When steel and stone and rail and rod
Become the avenue of God—
A trump to shout His thunder through
To crown the work that man may do.

To be alive in such an age!
When man, impatient of his cage,
Thrills to the soul's immortal rage
For conquest—reaches goal on goal,
Travels the earth from pole to pole,
Garners the tempests and the tides
And on a Dream Triumphant rides.
When, hid within the lump of clay,
A light more terrible than day
Proclaims the presence of that Force
Which hurls the planets on their course,
    O age with wings
    O age that flings
A challenge to the very sky,
Where endless realms of conquest lie!
When, earth on tiptoe, strives to hear
The message of a sister sphere,
Yearning to reach the cosmic wires
That flash Infinity's desires.

To be alive in such an age!
That blunders forth its discontent
With futile creed and sacrament,
Yet craves to utter God's intent,
Seeing beneath the world's unrest
Creation's huge, untiring quest,
And through Tradition's broken crust
The flame of Truth's triumphant thrust,
Below the seething thought of man
The push of a stupendous Plan.
    O age of strife!
    O age of life!
When Progress rides her chariots high,
And on the borders of the sky
The signals of the century
Proclaim the things that are to be—
The rise of woman to her place,
The coming of a nobler race.
To be alive in such an age—
    To live in it,
    To give to it!
Rise, soul, from thy despairing knees.
What if thy lips have drunk the lees?
Fling forth thy sorrows to the wind
And link thy hope with humankind—
The passion of a larger claim
Will put thy puny grief to shame.
Breathe the world thought, do the world deed,
Think hugely of thy brother's need.
And what thy woe, and what thy weal?
Look to the work the times reveal!
Give thanks with all thy flaming heart—
Crave but to have in it a part.
Give thanks and clasp thy heritage—
To be alive in such an age!

Angela Morgan

WE NEVER KNOW HOW HIGH

We never know how high we are
  Till we are called to rise;
And then, if we are true to plan,
  Our statures touch the skies.

The heroism we recite
  Would be a daily thing,
Did not ourselves the cubits warp
  For fear to be a king.

Emily Dickinson

FROM *JULIUS CAESAR*

There is a tide in the affairs of men,
Which, taken at the flood, leads on to fortune;
Omitted, all the voyage of their life
Is bound in shallows and in miseries:
And we must take the current when it serves,
Or lose our ventures.

William Shakespeare

THE WINDS OF FATE

One ship drives east and another drives west
  With the selfsame winds that blow.
    'Tis the set of the sails
    And not the gales
  Which tells us the way to go.

Like the winds of the sea are the ways of fate,
  As we voyage along through life:
    'Tis the set of a soul
    That decides its goal,
  And not the calm or the strife.

Ella Wheeler Wilcox

112

III
JESUS CHRIST

10. *The Wonder of His Coming*

THE WHOLE YEAR CHRISTMAS

Oh, could we keep the Christmas thrill,
The goad of gladness and good-will,
The lift of laughter and the touch
Of kindled hands that utter much,
Not once a year, but all the time,
The melody of hearts in chime,
The impulse beautiful and kind,
Of soul to soul and mind to mind
That swings the world
And brings the world
On one great day of all the year
Close to God's treasure house of cheer . . .
Oh, could we keep the Christmas feast,
Even when goods and gold are least;
Here, 'mid our common, daily scenes,
Could we but live what Christmas means,
Not one day, but for every day
The miracle of wholesome play,
The spirit sweet, gift-giving, young,
From deepest wells of feeling sprung . . .

What a different world this world would be!
For we would see as children see,
If only a magic way were found
To make us children the whole year round!

Angela Morgan

IN THE BLEAK MIDWINTER

In the bleak midwinter,
Frosty wind made moan,
Earth stood hard as iron,
Water like a stone;
Snow had fallen, snow on snow,
Snow on snow,
In the bleak midwinter,
Long ago.

Our God, heaven cannot hold him,
Nor earth sustain;
Heaven and earth shall flee away,
When he comes to reign;
In the bleak midwinter
A stable place sufficed
The Lord God almighty,
Jesus Christ.

Angels and archangels
May have gathered there,
Cherubim and seraphim
Thronged the air;
But his mother only,
In her maiden bliss,
Worshipped the beloved
With a kiss.

What can I give him,
Poor as I am?
If I were a shepherd,
I would bring a lamb;
If I were a wise man,
I would do my part;
Yet what I can I give him—
Give my heart.

Christina Rossetti

THE COMING CHILD

Welcome! all Wonders in one sight!
　　Eternity shut in a span.
Summer in winter, day in night,
　　Heaven in earth, and God in man.
Great little one! whose all-embracing birth
　　Lifts earth to heaven, stoops heav'n to earth!

Richard Crashaw

THAT HOLY THING

They all were looking for a king
　　To slay their foes, and lift them high:
Thou cam'st a little baby thing
　　That made a woman cry.

O son of man, to right my lot
　　Nought but thy presence can avail;
Yet on the road thy wheels are not,
　　Nor on the sea thy sail!

My fancied ways why shouldst thou heed?
　　Thou com'st down thine own secret stair;
Com'st down to answer all my need,
　　Yea, every bygone prayer!

George Macdonald

ETERNAL CHRISTMAS

In the pure soul, although it sing or pray,
The Christ is born anew from day to day;
The life that knoweth Him shall bide apart
And keep eternal Christmas in the heart.

Elizabeth Stuart Phelps

117

THERE'S A SONG IN THE AIR!

There's a song in the air!
There's a star in the sky!
There's a mother's deep prayer
And a baby's low cry!
And the star rains its fire while the beautiful sing,
For the manger of Bethlehem cradles a King!

There's a tumult of joy
O'er the wonderful birth,
For the Virgin's sweet boy
Is the Lord of the earth.
Ay! the star rains its fire while the beautiful sing,
For the manger of Bethlehem cradles a King!

In the light of that star
Lie the ages impearled;
And that song from afar
Has swept over the world.
Every hearth is aflame, and the beautiful sing
In the homes of the nations that Jesus is King!

We rejoice in the light,
And we echo the song
That comes down thro' the night
From the heavenly throng.
Ay! we shout to the lovely evangel they bring,
And we greet in His cradle our Saviour and King!

J. G. Holland

FAR TRUMPETS BLOWING

A king might miss the guiding star,
A wise man's foot might stumble;
For Bethlehem is very far
From all except the humble.

But he who gets to Bethlehem
Shall hear the oxen lowing;
And, if he humbly kneel with them,
May catch far trumpets blowing.

Louis F. Benson

LET US KEEP CHRISTMAS

Whatever else be lost among the years,
Let us keep Christmas still a shining thing:
Whatever doubts assail us, or what fears,
Let us hold close one day, remembering
Its poignant meaning for the hearts of men.
Let us get back our childlike faith again.

Grace Noll Crowell

FROM *CHRISTMAS ANTIPHONES*

Thou whose birth on earth
    Angels sang to men,
While thy stars made mirth,
Saviour, at thy birth,
    This day born again;

As this night was bright
    With thy cradle-ray,
Very light of light,
Turn the wild world's night
    To thy perfect day.

*   *   *

Bid our peace increase,
    Thou that madest morn:
Bid oppressions cease;

Bid the night be peace;
Bid the day be born.

Algernon Charles Swinburne

CHRISTMAS AT BABBITT'S

On Christmas eve they filled the house, some fifty guests all told,
(O little Lord of Christmas, were you left out in the cold?)

And ate and sang, played cards and danced till early morning light.
(O little Lord of Christmas, did they think of you that night?)

Next morning came the presents on a glittering Christmas tree.
(O little Lord of Christmas, was there any gift for thee?)

The dinner was a Roman feast, and how those guests did eat!
(O little Lord of Christmas, were you hungry in the street?)

Then came some teas, a movie, and at night the last revue.
(O little Lord of Christmas, what had these to do with you?)

By midnight all were tired and cross and tumbled into bed.
(O little Lord of Christmas, did they think that you were dead?)

They all woke up with headaches and no joy in work or play.
(O little Lord of Christmas, did they mark your birth that day?)

The love, the joy were good, no doubt; the rest a pagan spree.
(O little Lord of Christmas, let us keep the day with Thee!)

Henry Hallam Tweedy

I SAW A STABLE

I saw a stable, low and very bare,
A little child in a manger.

120

The oxen knew Him, had Him in their care,
    To men He was a stranger.
The safety of the world was lying there,
    And the world's danger.

                    Mary Elizabeth Coleridge

SHALL I BE SILENT?

The shepherds sing; and shall I silent be?
    My God, no hymn for thee?
My soul's a shepherd, too; a flock it feeds
    Of thoughts and words and deeds:
The pasture is thy Word; the streams thy grace,
    Enriching all the place.

                    George Herbert

FROM *AUGURIES OF INNOCENCE*

God appears, and God is Light,
To those poor souls who dwell in Night;
But does a Human Form display
To those who dwell in realms of Day.

                    William Blake

CHRISTMAS EVE

The door is on the latch tonight,
    The hearth-fire is aglow,
I seem to hear soft passing feet—
    The Christchild in the snow.

My heart is open wide tonight
    For stranger, kith or kin;
I would not bar a single door
    Where love might enter in.

                    Author unknown

11. *His Childhood and Youth*

THE LAMB

Little Lamb, who made thee?
 Dost thou know who made thee?
Gave thee life, and bid thee feed,
By the stream and o'er the mead;
Gave thee clothing of delight,
Softest clothing, woolly, bright;
Gave thee such a tender voice,
Making all the vales rejoice?
 Little Lamb, who made thee?
 Dost thou know who made thee?

Little Lamb, I'll tell thee,
 Little Lamb, I'll tell thee:
He is callèd by thy name,
For He calls Himself a Lamb.
He is meek, and He is mild;
He became a little child.
I a child, and thou a lamb,
We are callèd by His name.
 Little Lamb, God bless thee!
 Little Lamb, God bless thee!

William Blake

OUT OF BOUNDS

A little Boy of heavenly birth,
 But far from home to-day,
Comes down to find His ball, the earth,
 That sin has cast away.
O comrades, let us one and all
Join in to get Him back His ball!

       John Banister Tabl

LITTLE JESUS

Little Jesus, wast Thou shy
Once, and just so small as I?
And what did it feel like to be
Out of Heaven, and just like me?
Didst Thou sometimes think of there,
And ask where all the angels were?
I should think that I would cry
For my house all made of sky;
I would look about the air,
And wonder where my angels were;
And at waking 'twould distress me—
Not an angel there to dress me!
Hadst Thou ever any toys,
Like us little girls and boys?
And didst Thou play in Heaven with all
The angels that were not too tall,
With stars for marbles? Did the things
Play *Can you see me?* through their wings?
And did Thy Mother let Thee spoil
Thy robes, with playing on *our* soil?
How nice to have them always new
In Heaven, because 'twas quite clean blue!

Didst Thou kneel at night to pray,
And didst Thou join Thy hands, this way?
And did they tire sometimes, being young,
And make the prayer seem very long?
And dost Thou like it best, that we
Should join our hands to pray to Thee?
I used to think, before I knew,
The prayer not said unless we do.
And did Thy Mother at the night
Kiss Thee, and fold the clothes in right?
And didst Thou feel quite good in bed,
Kissed, and sweet, and Thy prayers said?

Thou canst not have forgotten all
That it feels like to be small:
And Thou know'st I cannot pray
To Thee in my father's way—
When Thou wast so little, say,
Couldst Thou talk Thy Father's way?—
So, a little Child, come down
And hear a child's tongue like Thy own;
Take me by the hand and walk,
And listen to my baby-talk.
To Thy Father show my prayer
(He will look, Thou art so fair),
And say: "O Father, I, Thy Son,
Bring the prayer of a little one."

And He will smile, that children's tongue
Has not changed since Thou wast young!

Francis Thompson

CHILD

The young child, Christ, is straight and wise
And asks questions of the old men, questions
Found under running water for all children,

And found under shadows thrown on still waters
By tall trees looking downwards, old and gnarled,
Found to the eyes of children alone, untold,
Singing a low song in the loneliness.
And the young child, Christ, goes asking,
And the old men answer nothing, and only know love
For the young child, Christ, straight and wise.

Carl Sandburg

THE CARPENTER

O Lord, at Joseph's humble bench
    Thy hands did handle saw and plane;
Thy hammer nails did drive and clench,
    Avoiding knot and humouring grain.

Lord, might I be but as a saw,
    A plane, a chisel, in thy hand!—
No, Lord! I take it back in awe,
    Such prayer for me is far too grand.

I pray, O Master, let me lie,
    As on thy bench the favoured wood;
Thy saw, thy plane, thy chisel ply,
    And work me into something good.

No, no; ambition, holy-high,
    Urges for more than both to pray:
Come in, O gracious Force, I cry—
    O workman, share my shed of clay.

That I, at bench, or desk, or oar,
    With knife or needle, voice or pen,
As thou in Nazareth of yore,
    Shall do the Father's will again.

Thus fashioning a workman rare,
O Master, this shall be thy fee:
Home to thy Father thou shalt bear
Another child made like to thee.

George Macdonald

O YOUNG AND FEARLESS PROPHET

O young and fearless Prophet of ancient Galilee:
Thy life is still a summons to serve humanity,
To make our thoughts and actions less prone to please the
crowd,
To stand with humble courage for thee with hearts uncowed.

We marvel at the purpose that held thee to thy course,
While ever on the hilltop before thee loomed the cross;
Thy steadfast face set forward where love and duty shone,
While we betray so quickly and leave thee there alone.

O help us stand unswerving against war's bloody way,
Where hate and lust and falsehood hold back Christ's holy
sway;
Forbid such love of country as blinds us to his call
Who sets above the nation the brotherhood of all.

Create in us the splendor that dawns when hearts are kind,
That knows not race or station as boundaries of the mind;
That learns to value beauty in heart, or brain, or soul,
And longs to bind God's children into one perfect whole.

Stir up in us a protest against the greed of wealth,
While men go starved and hungry who plead for work and
health;
Whose wives and little children cry out for lack of bread,
Who spend their years o'erweighted beneath a gloomy dread.

O young and fearless Prophet, we need thy presence here,
    Amid our pride and glory to see thy face appear;
      Once more to hear thy challenge above our noisy day,
    Triumphantly to lead us along God's holy way.

S. Ralph Harlow

O MASTER-WORKMAN OF THE RACE

O Master-workman of the race,
    Thou Man of Galilee,
Who with the eyes of early youth
    Eternal things did see,
We thank Thee for Thy boyhood faith
    That shone Thy whole life through;
"Did ye not know it is My work
    My Father's work to do?"

O Carpenter of Nazareth,
    Builder of life divine,
Who shapest man to God's own law,
    Thyself the fair design,
Build us a tower of Christlike height,
    That we the land may view,
And see like Thee our noblest work
    Our Father's work to do.

O Thou who didst the vision send
    And give to each his task,
And with the task sufficient strength,
    Show us Thy will, we ask;
Give us a conscience bold and good,
    Give us a purpose true,
That it may be our highest joy,
    Our Father's work to do.

Jay T. Stocking

12. His Life and Ministry

THE CHRIST

The good intent of God became the Christ.
And lived on earth—the Living Love of God,
That men might draw to closer touch with heaven,
Since Christ in all the ways of man hath trod.

John Oxenham

AMID THE DIN OF EARTHLY STRIFE

Amid the din of earthly strife,
    Amid the busy crowd,
The whispers of eternal life
    Are lost in clamors loud;
When lo! I find a healing balm,
    The world grows dim to me;
My spirit rests in sudden calm
    With Him of Galilee.

I linger near Him in the throng,
    And listen to His voice;
I feel my weary soul grow strong,
    My saddened heart rejoice.
Amid the storms that darkly frown
    I hear His call to me,
And lay my heavy burden down
    With Him of Galilee.

Henry Warburton Hawkes

MY MASTER WAS SO VERY POOR

My Master was so very poor,
 A manger was His cradling place;
So very rich my Master was,
 Kings came from far to gain His grace.

My Master was so very poor,
 And with the poor He broke the bread;
So very rich my Master was,
 That multitudes by Him were fed.

My Master was so very poor,
 They nailed Him naked to a cross;
So very rich my Master was,
 He gave His all and knew no loss.

Harry Lee

BREAK THOU THE BREAD OF LIFE

Break Thou the bread of life,
 Dear Lord, to me,
As Thou didst break the loaves
 Beside the sea;
Beyond the sacred page
 I seek Thee, Lord;
My spirit pants for Thee, O living Word!

Bless Thou the truth, dear Lord,
 To me, to me,
As Thou didst bless the bread
 By Galilee;
Then shall all bondage cease,
 All fetters fall;
And I shall find my peace,
 My All-in-All.

Mary A. Lathbury

OUR MASTER

Immortal Love, forever full,
 Forever flowing free,
Forever shared, forever whole,
 A never-ebbing sea!

Our outward lips confess the name
 All other names above;
Love only knoweth whence it came,
 And comprehendeth love.

We may not climb the heavenly steeps
 To bring the Lord Christ down:
In vain we search the lowest deeps,
 For Him no depths can drown.

But warm, sweet, tender, even yet
 A present help is He;
And faith has still its Olivet,
 And love its Galilee.

The healing of His seamless dress
 Is by our beds of pain;
We touch Him in life's throng and press,
 And we are whole again.

Through Him the first fond prayers are said
 Our lips of childhood frame,
The last low whispers of our dead
 Are burdened with His name.

O Lord and Master of us all!
 Whate'er our name or sign,
We own Thy sway, we hear Thy call,
 We test our lives by Thine.

John Greenleaf Whittier

THOU WHO TAUGHT THE THRONGING PEOPLE

Thou who taught the thronging people
 By blue Galilee:
Speak to us, Thy erring children,
 Teach us purity.

Thou whose touch could heal the leper,
 Make the blind to see:
Touch our hearts and turn the sinning
 Into purity.

Thou whose word could still the tempest,
 Calm the raging sea:
Hush the storm of human passion,
 Give us purity.

Thou who sinless met the tempter:
 Grant, O Christ, that we
May o'ercome the bent to evil
 By Thy purity.

Henry S. Minde

CHILDREN IN THE MARKET-PLACE

They are like children in the market-place.—LUKE 7:32

Like children in the market-place
 Who weary of their play,
We turn from folly's idle race
 And come to Thee today.
O Jesus, teller of the tale
 That never will grow old,
Thy words of living truth prevail
 Our listening hearts to hold.

Tell us of Father-love that speaks
   Peace to the wandering child;
Of valiant Shepherd-love that seeks
   The lost sheep in the wild;
Of deep Redeemer-love that knows
   What sins we need forgiven,
And on the Magdalen bestows
   The purest joy of Heaven.

Tell us of faith that's like a sword,
   And hope that's like a star;
How great the patient soul's reward,
   How blest the loyal are.
Tell us of courage like a wall
   No storm can batter down;
Tell us of men who venture all
   For Thee, and win a crown.

Tell us that life is not a game,
   But real and brave and true;
A journey with a glorious aim,
   A quest to carry through.
Tell us that though our wills are weak
   And though we children be,
The everlasting good we seek
   We can attain through Thee.

Henry van Dyke

IF CHRIST WERE HERE TO-NIGHT

If Christ were here to-night, and saw me tired,
   And half afraid another step to take,
I think He'd know the thing my heart desired,
   And ease that heart of all its throbbing ache.

If Christ were here in this dull room of mine,
  That gathers up so many shadows dim,
I am quite sure its narrow space would shine,
  And kindle into glory around Him.

If Christ were here, I might not pray so long;
  My prayer would have such little way to go;
'Twould break into a burst of happy song,
  So would my joy and gladness overflow.

If Christ were here to-night, I'd touch the hem
  Of his fair, seamless robe, and stand complete
In wholeness and in whiteness; I, who stem
  Such waves of pain, to kneel at His dear feet.

If Christ were here to-night, I'd tell Him all
  The load I carry for the ones I love—
The blinded ones, who grope and faint and fall,
  Following false guides, nor seeking Christ above.

If Christ were here! Ah, faithless soul and weak,
  Is not the Master ever close to thee?
Deaf is thine ear, that canst not hear Him speak;
  Dim is thine eye, His face that cannot see.

Thy Christ is here, and never far away;
  He entered with thee when thou camest in;
His strength was thine through all the busy day;
  He knew thy need, He kept thee pure from sin.

Thy blessèd Christ is in thy little room,
  Nay more, the Christ Himself is in thy heart;
Fear not, the dawn will scatter darkest gloom,
  And heaven will be of thy rich life a part.

Margaret E. Sangster

DEAR MASTER, IN WHOSE LIFE I SEE

Dear Master, in whose life I see
All that I would, but fail, to be,
Let thy clear light forever shine,
To shame and guide this life of mine.

Though what I dream and what I do
In all my days are often two,
Help me, oppressed by things undone,
O thou whose deeds and dreams were one.

John Hunter

COMFORTED

A great wind blowing, raging sea,
And rowers toiling wearily,
Far from the land where they would be.

And then One coming, drawing nigh;
They care not now for starless sky.
The Light of life says *It is I.*

They care not now for toil of oar,
For lo, the ship is at the shore,
And their Beloved they adore.

Lord of the Lake of Galilee,
Who long ago walked on the sea,
My heart is comforted in Thee.

Amy Carmichael

THE CARPENTER OF GALILEE

The Carpenter of Galilee
Comes down the street again,
In every land, in every age,
He still is building men.
On Christmas Eve we hear Him knock;
He goes from door to door:
"Are any workmen out of work?
The Carpenter needs more."

Hilda W. Smith

THE MAN CHRIST

He built no temple, yet the farthest sea
Can yield no shore that's barren of His place
    For bended knee.

He wrote no book, and yet His words and prayer
Are intimate on many myriad tongues,
    Are counsel everywhere.

The life He lived has never been assailed,
Nor any precept, as He lived it, yet
    Has ever failed.

He built no kingdom, yet a King from youth
He reigned, is reigning yet; they call His realm
    The kingdom of the Truth.

Therese Lindsey

FROM THE CRYSTAL

Oh, what amiss may I forgive in Thee,
Jesus, good Paragon, thou Crystal Christ?

Sidney Lanier

135

13.   His Suffering and Sacrifice

A BALLAD OF TREES AND THE MASTER

Into the woods my Master went,
Clean forspent, forspent.
Into the woods my Master came,
Forspent with love and shame.
But the olives they were not blind to Him,
The little gray leaves were kind to Him:
The thorn-tree had a mind to Him
When into the woods He came.

Out of the woods my Master went,
And He was well content.
Out of the woods my Master came,
Content with death and shame.
When Death and Shame would woo Him last,
From under the trees they drew Him last:
'Twas on a tree they slew Him—last
When out of the woods He came.

Sidney Lanier

BETRAYAL

Still as of old
Men by themselves are priced—
For thirty pieces Judas sold
Himself, not Christ.

Hester H. Cholmondeley

GOOD FRIDAY

Am I a stone, and not a sheep,
    That I can stand, O Christ, beneath Thy cross,
    To number drop by drop Thy Blood's slow loss,
And yet not weep?

Not so those women loved
    Who with exceeding grief laménted Thee;
    Not so fallen Peter weeping bitterly;
Not so the thief was moved;

Not so the Sun and Moon
    Which hid their faces in a starless sky.
    A horror of great darkness at broad noon—
I, only I.

Yet give not o'er
    But seek Thy sheep, true Shepherd of the flock;
    Greater than Moses, turn and look once more
And smite a rock.

Christina Rossetti

A THOUGHT

He who died on Calvary,
Died to ransom you and me.

On the cross He bowed His head,
In the grave He made His bed.

Ever since, the lilies bloom
Round the portal of the tomb.

Ever since, o'er all our loss
Shines the glory of the cross.

Margaret E. Sangster

LOVE IS OF GOD

Beloved, let us love: love is of God;
In God alone hath love its true abode.

Beloved, let us love: for they who love,
They only, are His sons, born from above.

Beloved, let us love: for love is rest,
And he who loveth not abides unblest.

Beloved, let us love: for love is light,
And he who loveth not dwelleth in night.

Beloved, let us love: for only thus
Shall we behold that God who loveth us.

Horatius Bonar

FROM *WITHIN AND WITHOUT*

Lord of Thyself and me, through the sore grief
Which Thou didst bear to bring us back to God,
Or, rather, bear in being unto us
Thy own pure shining self of love and truth!
When I have learnt to think Thy radiant thoughts,
To live the truth beyond the power to know it,
To bear my light as Thou Thy heavy cross,
Nor ever feel a martyr for Thy sake,
But an unprofitable servant still—
My highest sacrifice my simplest duty
Imperative and unavoidable,
Less than which *all* were nothingness and waste;
When I have lost myself in other men,
And found myself in Thee—the Father then
Will come with Thee, and will abide with me.

George Macdonald

138

ABOVE THE HILLS OF TIME

Above the hills of time the Cross is gleaming,
 Fair as the sun when night has turned to day;
And from it love's pure light is richly streaming,
 To cleanse the heart and banish sin away.
To this dear Cross the eyes of men are turning
 To-day as in the ages lost to sight;
And for the love of Christ men's hearts are yearning
 As shipwrecked seamen yearn for morning light.

The Cross, O Christ, Thy wondrous love revealing,
 Awakes our hearts as with the light of morn,
And pardon o'er our sinful spirits stealing
 Tells us that we, in Thee, have been re-born.
Like echoes to sweet temple bells replying,
 Our hearts, O Lord, make answer to Thy love;
And we will love Thee with a love undying,
 Till we are gathered to Thy home above.

Thomas Tiplady

TO KEEP A TRUE LENT

Is this a Fast, to keep
 The larder lean,
  And clean
From fat of veals and sheep?

Is it to quit the dish
 Of flesh, yet still
  To fill
The platter high with fish?

Is it to fast an hour,
 Or ragg'd to go,
  Or show
A downcast look and sour?

139

No: 'tis a Fast to dole
    Thy sheaf of wheat
        And meat,
Unto the hungry soul.

It is to fast from strife,
    From old debate
        And hate;
To circumcise thy life.

To show a heart grief-rent;
    To starve thy sin,
        Not bin:
And that's to keep thy Lent.

Robert Herrick

WIDE OPEN ARE THY LOVING HANDS

Wide open are Thy loving hands
    To pay with more than gold
The awful debt of guilty men,
    Forever and of old.

Ah, let me grasp those pierced hands,
    That we may never part,
And let the power of their blood
    Sustain my fainting heart.

Wide open are Thy saving arms,
    A fallen world t'embrace;
To take to love and endless rest
    Our whole forsaken race.

Lord, I am helpless, sad, and poor,
    But boundless is Thy grace;
Give me the soul-transforming joy
    For which I seek Thy face.

Draw all my mind, my soul, and heart
   Up to thy throne on high,
And let Thy sacred cross exalt
   My spirit to the sky.

To these, Thy mighty, faithful hands,
   My spirit I resign;
In life, I live alone to Thee,
   In death, alone am Thine.

Bernard of Clairvaux
(translated by C. P. Krauth)

I SEE HIS BLOOD UPON THE ROSE

I see His blood upon the rose
   And in the stars the glory of His eyes,
His Body gleams amid eternal snows,
   His tears fall from the skies.

I see His face in every flower;
   The thunder and the singing of the birds
Are but His voice—and carven by His power
   Rocks are His written words.

All pathways by His feet are worn,
   His strong heart stirs the ever-beating sea,
His crown of thorns is twined with every thorn,
   His cross is every tree.

Joseph Mary Plunkett

TO SEARCH OUR SOULS

To search our souls
To meditate
Will not suffice
For Lent.

141

To share the cross,
To sacrifice,
These are the things
God meant.

Jane McKay Lanning

HIS HANDS

The hands of Christ
  Seem very frail
For they were broken
  By a nail.

But only they
  Reach heaven at last
Whom these frail, broken
  Hands hold fast.

John Richard Moreland

WE MAY NOT KNOW

We may not know, we cannot tell what pains He had to bear,
But we believe it was for us He hung and suffered there.

Cecil F. Alexander

IN THINE OWN HEART

Though Christ a thousand times
  In Bethlehem be born,
If He's not born in thee
  Thy soul is still forlorn.
The cross on Golgotha
  Will never save thy soul,
The cross in thine own heart
  Alone can make thee whole.

Angelus Silesius

142

THERE IS A MAN ON THE CROSS

Whenever there is silence around me
By day or by night—
I am startled by a cry.
It came down from the cross—
The first time I heard it.
I went out and searched—
And found a man in the throes of crucifixion,
And I said, "I will take you down,"
And I tried to take the nails out of his feet.
But he said, "Let them be
For I cannot be taken down
Until every man, every woman, and every child
Come together to take me down."
And I said, "But I cannot hear you cry.
What can I do?"
And he said, "Go about the world—
Tell everyone that you meet—
There is a man on the cross."

Elizabeth Cheney

YET LISTEN NOW

Yet listen now,
Oh, listen with the wondering olive trees,
And the white moon that looked between the leaves,
And gentle earth that shuddered as she felt
Great drops of blood. All torturing questions find
Answer beneath those old grey olive trees.
There, only there, we can take heart to hope
For all lost lambs—Aye, even for ravening wolves.
Oh, there are things done in the world today
Would root up faith, but for Gethsemane.

For Calvary interprets human life;
   No path of pain but there we meet our Lord;
And all the strain, the terror and the strife
   Die down like waves before His peaceful word,
And nowhere but beside the awful Cross,
   And where the olives grow along the hill,
Can we accept the unexplained, the loss,
   The crushing agony, and hold us still.

Amy Carmichael

GOD WAS IN CHRIST

And all things are of God,
Who hath reconciled us to himself by Jesus Christ,
And hath given to us the ministry of reconciliation,
To wit, that God was in Christ,
Reconciling the world unto himself,
Not imputing their trespasses unto them,
And hath committed unto us the word of reconciliation.
Now then we are ambassadors for Christ,
As though God did beseech you by us;
We pray you in Christ's stead,
That ye be reconciled to God.
For he hath made him to be sin for us,
Who knew no sin,
That we might be made the righteousness of God in him.

Paul (II Corinthians 5:18-21)

BY HIM

What comfort by Him do we win
Who made Himself the price of sin
   To make us heirs of glory?
To see this Babe, all innocence,
A Martyr born in our defence:
   Can man forget this Story?

Ben Jonson

14. The Risen Lord

OUR CHRIST

I know not how that Bethlehem's Babe
    Could in the God-head be;
I only know the Manger Child
    Has brought God's life to me.

I know not how that Calvary's cross
    A world from sin could free:
I only know its matchless love
    Has brought God's love to me.

I know not how that Joseph's tomb
    Could solve death's mystery:
I only know a living Christ,
    Our immortality.

Harry Webb Farrington

EASTER

I got me flowers to straw Thy way,
I got me boughs off many a tree;
But Thou wast up by break of day,
And brought'st Thy sweets along with Thee.

Yet though my flowers be lost, they say
A heart can never come too late;
Teach it to sing Thy praise this day,
And then this day my life shall date.

George Herbert

EASTER HYMN

Christ the Lord is risen today,
   Sons of men and angels say:
Raise your joys and triumphs high,
   Sing, ye heavens, and earth reply.

Love's redeeming work is done,
   Fought the fight, the battle won;
Lo! our Sun's eclipse is o'er;
   Lo! He sets in blood no more.

Vain the stone, the watch, the seal;
   Christ hath burst the gates of hell!
Death in vain forbids His rise;
   Christ hath opened Paradise!

Lives again our glorious King:
   Where, O Death, is now thy sting?
Once He died, our souls to save:
   Where thy victory, O Grave?

Charles Wesley

AN EASTER SONG

A song of sunshine through the rain,
Of Spring across the snow;
A balm to heal the hurts of pain,
A peace surpassing woe.
Lift up your heads, ye sorrowing ones,
And be ye glad at heart,
For Calvary and Easter Day,
Earth's saddest day and gladdest day,
Were just three days apart!

Susan Coolidge

146

IF EASTER BE NOT TRUE

If Easter be not true,
Then all the lilies low must lie:
The Flanders poppies fade and die;
The spring must lose her fairest bloom
For Christ were still within the tomb—
    If Easter be not true.

If Easter be not true,
Then faith must mount on broken wing;
Then hope no more immortal spring;
Then love must lose her mighty urge;
Life prove a phantom, death a dirge—
    If Easter be not true.

If Easter be not true,
'Twere foolishness the cross to bear;
He died in vain who suffered there;
What matter though we laugh or cry,
Be good or evil, live or die,
    If Easter be not true?

If Easter be not true—
But it is true, and Christ is risen!
And mortal spirit from its prison
Of sin and death with him may rise!
Worthwhile the struggle, sure the prize,
    Since Easter, aye, is true!

                                Henry H. Barstow

THE HEAD THAT ONCE WAS CROWNED
WITH THORNS

The head that once was crowned with thorns
Is crowned with glory now;

A royal diadem adorns
The mighty victor's brow.

The highest place that heaven affords
Is his, is his by right;
The King of kings, and Lord of lords,
And heaven's eternal light.

The joy of all who dwell above,
The joy of all below,
To whom he manifests his love,
And grants his name to know.

To them the cross, with all its shame,
With all its grace, is given;
Their name an everlasting name,
Their joy the joy of heaven.

Thomas Kelly

EASTER MORNING

Most glorious Lord of life, that on this day
Didst make thy triumph over death and sin,
And, having harrowed hell, didst bring away
Captivity thence captive, us to win;
This joyous day, dear Lord, with joy begin,
And grant that we, for whom thou didst die,
Being with thy dear blood clean washed from sin,
May live forever in felicity:
And that thy love we weighing worthily,
May likewise love thee for the same again:
And for thy sake, that all like dear didst buy,
With love may one another entertain.
So let us love, dear love, like as we ought;
Love is the lesson which the Lord us taught.

Edmund Spenser

BLESSING, AND HONOR

Blessing, and honor, and glory, and power,
    Wisdom, and riches, and strength evermore,
Give ye to Him who our battle hath won,
    Whose are the Kingdom, the crown, and the throne.

Dwelleth the light of the glory with Him,
    Light of a glory that cannot grow dim,
Light in its silence and beauty and calm,
    Light in its gladness and brightness and balm.

Ever ascendeth the song and the joy,
    Ever descendeth the love from on high,
Blessing, and honor, and glory, and praise,
    This is the theme of the hymns that we raise.

Life of all life, and true Light of all light,
    Star of the dawning, unchangingly bright,
Sing we the song of the Lamb that was slain,
    Dying in weakness, but rising to reign.

Horatius Bonar

GRACE AT EVENING

Be with us, Lord, at eventide;
    Far has declined the day,
Our hearts have glowed
Along the road,
    Thou hast made glad our way.

Take Thou this loaf and bless it, Lord,
    And then with us partake;
Unveil our eyes
To recognize
    Thyself, for Thy dear sake.

Edwin McNeill Poteat
149

15.   *Our Saviour and Our Friend*

HYMN OF LABOR

Jesus, Thou divine Companion,
   By Thy lowly human birth
Thou hast come to join the workers,
   Burden-bearers of the earth.
Thou, the Carpenter of Naz'reth,
   Toiling for Thy daily food,
By Thy patience and Thy courage,
   Thou hast taught us toil is good.

They who tread the path of labor
   Follow where Thy feet have trod;
They who work without complaining
   Do the holy will of God.
Thou, the peace that passeth knowledge,
   Dwellest in the daily strife;
Thou, the Bread of heaven, art broken
   In the sacrament of life.

Every task, however simple,
   Sets the soul that does it free;
Every deed of love and kindness
   Done to man is done to Thee.
Jesus, Thou divine Companion,
   Help us all to work our best;
Bless us in our daily labor,
   Lead us to our Sabbath rest.

Henry van Dyke

FROM *THE EVERLASTING MERCY*

O Christ who holds the open gate,
O Christ who drives the furrow straight,
O Christ, the plough, O Christ, the laughter
Of holy white birds flying after,
Lo, all my heart's field red and torn,
And Thou wilt bring young green corn,
The young green corn divinely springing,
The young green corn forever singing;
And when the field is fresh and fair
Thy blessed feet shall glitter there.
And we will walk the weeded field,
And tell the golden harvest's yield,
The corn that makes the holy bread
By which the soul of man is fed,
The holy bread, the food unpriced,
Thy everlasting mercy, Christ.

John Masefield

NONE OTHER LAMB

None other Lamb, none other Name,
    None other Hope in heaven or earth or sea,
None other Hiding-place from guilt and shame,
    None beside Thee.

My faith burns low, my hope burns low
    Only my heart's desire cries out in me
By the deep thunder of its want and woe
    Cries out to Thee.

Lord, Thou art Life tho' I be dead,
    Love's Fire Thou art, however cold I be:
Nor heaven have I, nor place to lay my head,
    Nor home, but Thee.

Christina Rossetti

151

A VIRILE CHRIST

Give us a virile Christ for these rough days!
You painters, sculptors, show the warrior bold;
And you who turn mere words to gleaming gold,
Too long your lips have sounded in the praise
Of patience and humility. Our ways
Have parted from the quietude of old;
We need a man of strength with us to hold
The very breach of Death without amaze.
Did he not scourge from temple courts the thieves?
And make the arch-fiend's self again to fall?
And blast the fig tree that was only leaves?
And still the raging tumult of the seas?
Did he not bear the greatest pain of all,
Silent, upon the cross on Calvary?

Rex Boundy

HE THAT IS NEAR ME IS NEAR THE FIRE

The Savior Himself says:
"He that is near Me is near the fire.
He that is far from Me is far from the Kingdom."

Origen

HE IS A PATH

He is a path, if any be misled;
He is a robe, if any naked be;
If any chance to hunger, He is bread;
If any be a bondman, He is free;
If any be but weak, how strong is He!
To dead men, life is He; to sick men, health;
To blind men, sight; and to the needy, wealth;
A pleasure without loss; a treasure without stealth.

Giles Fletcher

APPROACHES

When thou turn'st away from ill,
Christ is this side of thy hill.

When thou turnest toward good,
Christ is walking in thy wood.

When thy heart says, "Father, pardon!"
Then the Lord is in thy garden.

When stern Duty wakes to watch,
Then His hand is on the latch.

But when Hope thy song doth rouse,
Then the Lord is in the house.

When to love is all thy wit,
Christ doth at thy table sit.

When God's will is thy heart's pole,
Then is Christ thy very soul.

George Macdonald

THE SONG OF A HEATHEN

If Jesus Christ is a man—
    And only a man,—I say
That of all mankind I cleave to him,
    And to him will I cleave alway.

If Jesus Christ is a God—
    And the only God,—I swear
I will follow him through heaven and hell,
    The earth, the sea, the air!

Richard Watson Gilder

153

I AM THE WAY

Thou art the Way.
Hadst Thou been nothing but the goal,
I cannot say
If Thou hadst ever met my soul.

I cannot see—
I, child of process—if there lies
An end for me,
Full of repose, full of replies.

I'll not reproach
The road that winds, my feet that err.
Access, approach
Art Thou, Time, Way, and Wayfarer.

Alice Meynell

NO COMING TO GOD WITHOUT CHRIST

Good and great God! How should I fear
To come to Thee, if Christ not there!
Could I but think, He would not be
Present, to plead my cause for me;
To Hell I'd rather run, than I
Would see Thy face, and He not by.

Robert Herrick

FROM *IN MEMORIAM*

Strong Son of God, immortal Love,
    Whom we, that have not seen thy face,
    By faith, and faith alone, embrace,
Believing where we cannot prove;

154

Thine are these orbs of light and shade;
   Thou madest Life in man and brute;
   Thou madest Death; and lo, thy foot
Is on the skull which thou hast made.

Thou wilt not leave us in the dust:
   Thou madest man, he knows not why;
   He thinks he was not made to die;
And thou hast made him: thou art just.

Thou seemest human and divine,
   The highest, holiest manhood, thou:
   Our wills are ours, we know not how;
Our wills are ours, to make them thine.

Alfred Tennyson

FROM *SAUL*

He who did most, shall bear most; the strongest shall stand the
   most weak.
'Tis the weakness in strength, that I cry for! my flesh, that I seek
In the Godhead! I seek and I find it. O Saul, it shall be
A Face like my face that receives thee; a Man like to me,
Thou shalt love and be loved by, forever: a Hand like this hand
Shall throw open the gates of new life to thee! See the Christ stand!

Robert Browning

FROM *SAINT PAUL*

Christ! I am Christ's! and let the name suffice you,
   Ay, for me too He greatly hath sufficed;
Lo with no winning words I would entice you,
   Paul has no honour and no friend but Christ.

155

Yes, without cheer of sister or of daughter,
   Yes, without stay of father or of son,
Lone on the land and homeless on the water
   Pass I in patience till the work be done.

Yet not in solitude if Christ anear me
   Waketh Him workers for the great employ,
Oh not in solitude, if souls that hear me
   Catch from my joyance the surprise of joy.

Yea thro' life, death, thro' sorrow and thro' sinning
   He shall suffice me, for He hath sufficed:
Christ is the end, for Christ was the beginning,
   Christ the beginning, for the end is Christ.

Frederic W. H. Myers

FROM *ST. PATRICK*

Christ with me, Christ before me, Christ behind me,
Christ in me, Christ beneath me, Christ above me,
Christ on my right, Christ on my left,
Christ in breadth, Christ in length, Christ in height,
Christ in the heart of every man who thinks of me,
Christ in the mouth of everyone who speaks of me,
Christ in every eye that sees me,
Christ in every ear that hears me.

Phyllis Garlick

JESUS AND I

I can not do it alone;
   The waves run fast and high,
And the fogs close chill around,
   And the light goes out in the sky;
But I know that we two shall win in the end—
   Jesus and I.

156

I can not row it myself,
  My boat on the raging sea;
But beside me sits Another,
  Who pulls or steers with me;
And I know that we too shall come into port—
  His child and He.

Coward and wayward and weak,
  I change with the changing sky,
To-day so eager and brave,
  To-morrow not caring to try;
But He never gives in, so we two shall win—
  Jesus and I.

Dan Crawford

FAIREST LORD JESUS

Fairest Lord Jesus,
  Ruler of all nature,
O thou of God and man the Son;
  Thee will I cherish, thee will I honour,
Thou, my soul's glory, joy, and crown.

Fair are the meadows,
  Fairer still the woodlands,
Robed in the blooming garb of spring:
  Jesus is fairer, Jesus is purer,
Who makes the woeful heart to sing.

Fair is the sunshine,
  Fairer still the moonlight,
And all the twinkling, starry host:
  Jesus shines brighter, Jesus shines purer,
Then all the angels heaven can boast.

Author unknown

PAUL

Bond-slave to Christ, and in my bonds rejoicing,
  Earmarked to Him I counted less than nought;
His man henceforward, eager to be voicing
  That wondrous Love which Saul the Roman sought.

Sought him and found him, working bitter sorrow;
  Found him and claimed him, chose him for His own;
Bound him in darkness, till the glorious morrow
  Unsealed his eyes to that he had not known.

John Oxenham

HIM EVERMORE I BEHOLD

Him evermore I behold
Walking in Galilee,
Through the cornfield's waving gold,
In hamlet or grassy wold,
By the shores of the Beautiful Sea.
He toucheth the sightless eyes;
Before Him the demons flee;
To the dead He sayeth: Arise!
To the living: Follow me!
And that voice still soundeth on
From the centuries that are gone,
To the centuries that shall be!

Henry Wadsworth Longfellow

IN SWEET COMMUNION

May the grace of Christ our Saviour,
  and the Father's boundless love,
With the Holy Spirit's favor, rest upon us from above.
Thus may we abide in union with each other and the Lord,
And possess in sweet communion joys which earth cannot afford.

John Newton

158

IV
THE LIFE
OF THE SPIRIT

16. Portals of Prayer

PROOF

If radio's slim fingers can pluck a melody
From night—and toss it over a continent or sea;
If the petalled white notes of a violin
Are blown across the mountains or the city's din;
If songs, like crimson roses, are culled from thin blue air—
Why should mortals wonder if God hears prayer?

Ethel Romig Fuller

TWO PRAYERS

Last night my little boy confessed to me
Some childish wrong;
And kneeling at my knee,
He prayed with tears—
"Dear God, make me a man
Like Daddy—wise and strong;
I know you can."

Then while he slept
I knelt beside his bed,
Confessed my sins,
And prayed with low-bowed head.
"O God, make me a child
Like my child here—
Pure, guileless,
Trusting Thee with faith sincere."

Andrew Gillies

THOU HAST MADE US FOR THYSELF

Thou hast made us for Thyself
And our hearts are restless until they rest in Thee.

St. Augustine of Hippo

FROM *IN MEMORIAM*

Are God and Nature then at strife,
    That Nature lends such evil dreams?
    So careful of the type she seems
So careless of the single life;

That I, considering everywhere
    Her secret meaning in her deeds,
    And finding that of fifty seeds
She often brings but one to bear,

I falter where I firmly trod,
    And falling with my weight of cares
    Upon the great world's altar-stairs
That slope thro' darkness up to God,

I stretch lame hands of faith, and grope,
    And gather dust and chaff, and call
    To what I feel is Lord of all,
And faintly trust the larger hope.

Alfred Tennyson

THOU ART COMING TO A KING

Thou art coming to a King,
Large petitions with thee bring
For His grace and power are such
None can ever ask too much.

John Newton

PRAYER

Lord, what a change within us one short hour
Spent in Thy presence will prevail to make!
What heavy burdens from our bosoms take,
What parched grounds refresh as with a shower!
We kneel, and all around us seems to lower;
We rise, and all, the distant and the near,
Stands forth in sunny outline brave and clear;
We kneel, how weak! we rise, how full of power!
Why, therefore, should we do ourselves this wrong
Or others, that we are not always strong,
That we are ever overborne with care,
That we should ever weak or heartless be,
Anxious or troubled, when with us is prayer,
And joy and strength and courage are with Thee!

Richard Chenevix Trench

FROM *MORTE D'ARTHUR*

The old order changeth, yielding place to new,
And God fulfils himself in many ways,
Lest one good custom should corrupt the world.
Comfort thyself: what comfort is in me?
I have lived my life, and that which I have done
May He within himself make pure! but thou,
If thou shouldst never see my face again,
Pray for my soul. More things are wrought by prayer
Than this world dreams of. Wherefore, let thy voice
Rise like a fountain for me night and day.
For what are men better than sheep or goats
That nourish a blind life within the brain,
If, knowing God, they lift not hands of prayer
Both for themselves and those who call them friend?
For so the whole round earth is every way
Bound by gold chains about the feet of God. . . .

Alfred Tennyson

163

TWO WENT UP TO THE TEMPLE TO PRAY

Two went to pray? Oh, rather say
One went to brag, the other to pray;
One stands up close and treads on high
Where the other dares not send his eye;
One nearer to God's altar trod,
The other to the altar's God.

Richard Crashaw

WHAT IS PRAYER?

Prayer is the soul's sincere desire,
    Uttered or unexpressed;
The motion of a hidden fire,
    That trembles in the breast.

Prayer is the burden of a sigh,
    The falling of a tear;
The upward glancing of an eye,
    When none but God is near.

Prayer is the simplest form of speech
    That infant lips can try;
Prayer, the sublimest strains that reach
    The Majesty on high.

Prayer is the contrite sinner's voice,
    Returning from his ways;
While angels in their songs rejoice,
    And cry, "Behold! He prays!"

Prayer is the Christian's vital breath,
    The Christian's native air;
His watchword at the gate of death—
    He enters heaven with prayer.

The saints in prayer appear as one
　　In word and deed and mind;
Where with the Father and the Son
　　Sweet fellowship they find.

Nor prayer is made by man alone:
　　The Holy Spirit pleads;
And Jesus, on the eternal Throne,
　　For sinners intercedes.

O Thou by whom we come to God—
　　The Life, the Truth, the Way!
The path of prayer Thyself hast trod;
　　Lord, teach us how to pray!

James Montgomery

PRAYER

Prayer, the Church's banquet, Angels' age,
　　God's breath in man returning to his birth,
The soul in paraphrase, heart in pilgrimage,
　　The Christian plummet sounding heav'n and earth;

Engine against th' Almighty, sinner's tower,
　　Reversèd thunder, Christ-side-piercing spear,
The six-days-world transposing in an hour,
　　A kind of tune which all things hear and fear;

Softness, and peace, and joy, and love, and bliss,
　　Exalted Manna, gladness of the best,
　　Heaven in ordinary, man well dressed,
The milky way, the bird of Paradise,

　　Church-bells beyond the stars heard, the soul's blood,
　　The land of spices, something understood.

George Herbert

165

FROM ANDREW RYKMAN'S PRAYER

If there be some weaker one,
Give me strength to help him on;
If a blinder soul there be,
Let me guide him nearer Thee.
Make my mortal dreams come true
With the work I fain would do;
Clothe with life the weak intent,
Let me be the thing I meant;
Let me find in Thy employ
Peace that dearer is than joy;
Out of self to love be led
And to heaven acclimated,
Until all things sweet and good
Seem my natural habitude.

John Greenleaf Whittier

INDIAN PRAYER

O Thou great mystery,
Creator of the universe,
Good and powerful as Thou art,
Whose powers are displayed in
The wonders of the sun and glories of the moon,
And the great foliage of the forest
And the great waters of the deep,
Sign of the four winds;
Whatever four corners of the earth that we may meet—
Let us be friends, pale face and red man,
And when we come to the end of that long trail,
And we step off into the happy hunting ground,
From which no hunter ever returns,
Let us not only have faith in Thee—O Thou great mystery—
But faith in each other.
O Thou Kitchi Manito, hear us!

Chief Joseph Strongwolf

WHIRRING WHEELS

Lord, when on my bed I lie,
Sleepless, unto Thee I'll cry;
When my brain works overmuch,
Stay the wheels with Thy soft touch.
Just a quiet thought of Thee,
And of Thy sweet charity,—
Just a little prayer, and then
I will turn to sleep again.

John Oxenham

ST. FRANCIS' PRAYER

Lord, make me an instrument of Thy peace.
Where there is hate, may I bring love;
Where offense, may I bring pardon;
May I bring union in place of discord;
Truth, replacing error;
Faith, where once there was doubt;
Hope, for despair;
Light, where was darkness;
Joy to replace sadness.
Make me not to so crave to be loved as to love.
Help me to learn that in giving I may receive;
In forgetting self, I may find life eternal.

St. Francis of Assisi

TO MY GOD

Oh how oft I wake and find
I have been forgetting thee!
I am never from thy mind:
Thou it is that wakest me.

George Macdonald
167

FOR ALL IN PAIN

Dear Lord, for all in pain
  We pray to Thee;
O come and smite again
  Thine enemy.

Give to Thy servants skill
  To soothe and bless,
And to the tired and ill
  Give quietness.

And, Lord, to those who know
  Pain may not cease,
Come near, that even so
  They may have peace.

Amy Carmichael

THE CELESTIAL SURGEON

If I have faltered more or less
In my great task of happiness:
If I have moved among my race
And shown no glorious morning face;
If beams from happy human eyes
Have moved me not; if morning skies,
Books, and my food, and summer rain
Knocked on my sullen heart in vain:—
Lord, thy most pointed pleasure take
And stab my spirit broad awake;
Or, Lord, if still too obdurate I,
Choose thou, before that spirit die,
A piercing pain, a killing sin,
And to my dead heart run them in!

Robert Louis Stevenson

168

AN OLD IRISH BLESSING

May the blessing of light be on you,
Light without and light within.
May the blessed sunshine shine on you
And warm your heart till it glows like a great peat fire,
So the stranger may come and warm himself at it,
And also a friend.

And may the light shine out of the two eyes of you
Like a candle set in two windows of a house,
Bidding the wanderer to come in out of the storm.

And may the blessing of the rain be on you—
The soft sweet rain.
May it fall upon your spirit
So that all the little flowers may spring up,
And shed their sweetness on the air.

And may the blessing of the earth be on you—
The great, round earth:
May you ever have a kindly greeting for them you pass
As you are going along the roads.
May the earth be soft under you when you rest upon it,
Tired at the end of the day,
And may it rest easy over you
When, at the last, you lay out under it.
May it rest so lightly over you
That your soul may be out from under it quickly—
And up and off and on its way to God.

Author unknown

GOD BE IN MY HEAD

God be in my head,
And in my understanding;
God be in my eyes,
And in my looking;

God be in my mouth,
And in my speaking;
God be in my heart,
And in my thinking;
God be at my end,
And at my departing.

Old Sarum Primer

A GRACE

Reveal Thy Presence now, O Lord,
As in the Upper Room of old;
Break Thou our bread, grace Thou our board,
And keep our hearts from growing cold.

Thomas Tiplady

PRAYER FOR STRENGTH

Father, in Thy mysterious presence kneeling,
Fain would our souls feel all Thy kindling love;
For we are weak, and need some deep revealing
Of trust and strength and calmness from above.

Lord, we have wandered forth through doubt and sorrow,
And Thou hast made each step an onward one;
And we will ever trust each unknown morrow,—
Thou wilt sustain us till its work is done.

In the heart's depths a peace serene and holy
Abides; and when pain seems to have its will,
Or we despair, O may that peace rise slowly,
Stronger than agony, and we be still!

Now, Father, now, in Thy dear presence kneeling,
Our spirits yearn to feel Thy kindling love:
Now make us strong, we need Thy deep revealing
Of trust and strength and calmness from above.

Samuel Johnson

170

PROPS

Earthly props are useless,
    On Thy grace I fall;
Earthly strength is weakness,
    Father, on Thee I call—
    For comfort, strength, and guidance,
    O, give me all!

John Oxenham

LORD, THOU HAST SUFFERED

Lord, Thou hast suffered, Thou dost know
The thrust of pain, the piercing dart,
How wearily the wind can blow
Upon the tired heart.

He whom Thou lovest, Lord, is ill.
O come, Thou mighty Vanquisher
Of wind and wave, say, Peace, be still,
Eternal Comforter.

Amy Carmichael

GIVE TO THE WINDS THY FEARS

Give to the winds thy fears;
    Hope and be undismayed:
God hears thy sighs and counts thy tears;
    God shall lift up thy head.

Through waves, and clouds, and storms,
    He gently clears thy way;
Wait thou His time: so shall this night
    Soon end in joyous day.

Leave to His sovereign sway
   To choose and to command;
So shalt thou, wondering, own His way
   How wise, how strong His hand!

Far, far above thy thought
   His counsel shall appear,
When fully He the work hath wrought
   That caused thy needless fear.

Paul Gerhardt (translated by John Wesley)

TO THE SUPREME BEING

The prayers I make will then be sweet indeed
If Thou the spirit give by which I pray:
My unassisted heart is barren clay,
That of its native self can nothing feed:
Of good and pious works Thou art the seed,
That quickens only where Thou say'st it may:
Unless Thou show to us Thine own true way
No man can find it: Father! Thou must lead.
Do Thou, then, breathe those thoughts into my mind
By which such virtue may in me be bred
That in Thy holy footsteps I may tread;
The fetters of my tongue do Thou unbind,
That I may have the power to sing of Thee,
And sound Thy praises everlastingly.

Michelangelo (translated by William Wordsworth)

HELP US TO LIVE

Only, O Lord, in Thy dear love
Fit us for perfect rest above;
And help us this and every day,
To live more nearly as we pray.

John Keble

17. Faith and Trust

FROM *THE PASSIONATE MAN'S PILGRIMAGE*

Give me my scallop shell of quiet,
My staff of faith to walk upon,
My scrip of joy, immortal diet,
My bottle of salvation:
My gown of glory, hope's true gage,
And thus I'll take my pilgrimage.

Blood must be my body's balmer,
No other balm will there be given,
Whilst my soul like a white palmer,
Travels to the land of heaven;
Over the silver mountains,
Where spring the nectar fountains:
And there I'll kiss
The bowl of bliss,
And drink my eternal fill
On every milken hill.
My soul will be a-dry before,
But after it will ne'er thirst more.

Sir Walter Raleigh

THE EVIDENCE

Now faith is the substance of things hoped for,
the evidence of things not seen.

Hebrews 11:1

FAITH

Nothing before, nothing behind;
    The steps of faith
Fall on the seeming void, and find
    The rock beneath.

John Greenleaf Whittier

FROM *IN MEMORIAM*

Perplext in faith, but pure in deeds,
    At last he beat his music out.
    There lives more faith in honest doubt,
Believe me, than in half the creeds.

He fought his doubts and gather'd strength,
    He would not make his judgment blind,
    He faced the specters of the mind
And laid them; thus he came at length

To find a stronger faith his own,
    And Power was with him in the night,
    Which makes the darkness and the light,
And dwells not in the light alone.

Alfred Tennyson

FAITH

God knows, not I, the reason why
    His winds of storm drive through my door;
I am content to live or die
    Just knowing this, nor knowing more.
My Father's hand appointing me
My days and ways, so I am free.

Margaret E. Sangster

174

O WORLD

O world, thou choosest not the better part!
It is not wisdom to be only wise,
And on the inward vision close the eyes;
But it is wisdom to believe the heart.
Columbus found a world, and had no chart
Save one that faith deciphered in the skies;
To trust the soul's invincible surmise
Was all his science and his only art.
Our knowledge is a torch of smoky pine
That lights the pathway but one step ahead
Across a void of mystery and dread.
Bid, then, the tender light of faith to shine
By which alone the mortal heart is led
Unto the thinking of the thought divine.

George Santayana

WHOSO DRAWS NIGH TO GOD

Whoso draws nigh to God one step through doubtings dim,
God will advance a mile in blazing light to him.

Author unknown

CHARTLESS

I never saw a moor,
I never saw the sea;
Yet know I how the heather looks,
And what a wave must be.

I never spoke with God,
Nor visited in Heaven;
Yet certain am I of the spot
As if the chart were given.

Emily Dickinson

175

POSSESSION

Heaven above is softer blue
    Earth beneath is sweeter green.
Something lives in every hue,
    Christless eyes have never seen.
Birds with gladder songs o'erflow,
    Flowers with deeper beauty shine
Since I know as now I know
    I am His and He is mine.

Author unknown

FAITH

I will not doubt, though all my ships at sea
    Come drifting home with broken masts and sails;
    I shall believe the Hand which never fails,
From seeming evil worketh good to me;
    And, though I weep because those sails are battered,
    Still will I cry, while my best hopes lie shattered,
        "I trust in Thee."

I will not doubt, though all my prayers return
    Unanswered from the still, white realm above;
    I shall believe it is an all-wise Love
Which has refused those things for which I yearn;
    And though, at times, I cannot keep from grieving,
    Yet the pure ardor of my fixed believing
        Undimmed shall burn.

I will not doubt, though sorrows fall like rain,
    And troubles swarm like bees about a hive;
    I shall believe the heights for which I strive,
Are only reached by anguish and by pain;
    And, though I groan and tremble with my crosses,
    I yet shall see, through my severest losses,
        The greater gain.

I will not doubt; well anchored in the faith,
  Like some stanch ship, my soul braves every gale,
  So strong its courage that it will not fail
To breast the mighty, unknown sea of death.
  Oh, may I cry when body parts with spirit,
    "I do not doubt," so listening worlds may hear it
      With my last breath.

Ella Wheeler Wilcox

THE POET'S SIMPLE FAITH

You say, "Where goest thou?" I cannot tell,
And still go on. If but the way be straight
I cannot go amiss: before me lies
Dawn and the day: the night behind me: that
Suffices me: I break the bounds: I see,
And nothing more; believe and nothing less.
My future is not one of my concerns.

Victor Hugo

A NOISELESS PATIENT SPIDER

A noiseless patient spider,
I mark'd where on a little promontory it stood isolated,
Mark'd how to explore the vacant vast surrounding,
It launch'd forth filament, filament, filament, out of itself.
Ever unreeling them, ever tirelessly speeding them.

And you O my soul where you stand,
Surrounded, detached, in measureless oceans of space,
Ceaselessly musing, venturing, throwing, seeking the spheres
    to connect them,
Till the bridge you will need be form'd, till the ductile
    anchor hold,
Till the gossamer thread you fling catch somewhere, O my soul.

Walt Whitman

THE FAITH OF ABRAHAM LINCOLN

I believe the will of God prevails;
Without Him all human reliance is vain;
Without the assistance of that Divine Being I cannot succeed;
With that assistance I cannot fail.
 I believe I am a humble instrument in the hands
   of our Heavenly Father;
I desire that all my works and acts be according to His will;
And that it may be so I give thanks to the Almighty
   and seek His aid.

   Abraham Lincoln (formulated by Carl Sandburg from
      Lincoln's own words; from *The War Years*)

OVERHEARD IN AN ORCHARD

Said the Robin to the Sparrow:
 "I should really like to know
Why these anxious human beings
 Rush about and worry so."

Said the Sparrow to the Robin:
 "Friend, I think that it must be
That they have no heavenly Father
 Such as cares for you and me."

        Elizabeth Cheney

ENCOURAGED

Because you love me I have much achieved,
Had you despised me then I must have failed,
But since I knew you trusted and believed,
I could not disappoint you and so prevailed.

       Paul Laurence Dunbar

178

LIFE AND LOVE

Yet Love will dream and Faith will trust,
Since He who knows our need is just,
That somewhere, somehow, meet we must.
Alas for him who never sees
The stars shine through his cypress-trees;
Who hopeless lays his dead away,
Nor looks to see the breaking day
Across the mournful marbles play;
Who hath not learned, in hours of faith,
The truth to flesh and sense unknown,
That life is ever lord of death,
And love can never lose its own!

John Greenleaf Whittier

VOYAGERS' PRAYER

O Great Spirit!
Thou hast made this lake;
Thou hast also created us as Thy children;
Thou art able to make this water calm
Until we have safely passed over.

Chippewa Indians

FAITH

In every seed to breathe the flower,
In every drop of dew
To reverence a cloistered star
Within the distant blue;
To wait the promise of the bow
Despite the cloud between,
Is Faith—the fervid evidence
Of loveliness unseen.

John Banister Tabb

179

THE TIDE OF FAITH

So faith is strong
Only when we are strong, shrinks when we shrink.
It comes when music stirs us, and the chords,
Moving on some grand climax, shake our souls
With influx new that makes new energies.
It comes in swellings of the heart and tears
That rise at noble and at gentle deeds.
It comes in moments of heroic love,
Unjealous joy in joy not made for us;
In conscious triumph of the good within,
Making us worship goodness that rebukes.
Even our failures are a prophecy,
Even our yearnings and our bitter tears
After that fair and true we cannot grasp.
Presentiment of better things on earth
Sweeps in with every force that stirs our souls
To admiration, self-renouncing love.

George Eliot

THE KINGDOM OF GOD

O world invisible, we view thee,
O world intangible, we touch thee,
O world unknowable, we know thee,
Inapprehensible, we clutch thee!

Does the fish soar to find the ocean,
The eagle plunge to find the air—
That we ask of the stars in motion
If they have rumour of thee there?

Not where the wheeling systems darken,
And our benumbed conceiving soars!—
The drift of pinions, would we hearken,
Beats at our own clay-shuttered doors.

The angels keep their ancient places;—
Turn but a stone, and start a wing!
'Tis ye, 'tis your estrangèd faces,
That miss the many-splendoured thing.

But (when so sad thou canst not sadder)
Cry;—and upon thy so sore loss
Shall shine the traffic of Jacob's ladder
Pitched betwixt Heaven and Charing Cross.

Yes, in the night, my Soul, my daughter,
Cry,—clinging Heaven by the hems;
And lo, Christ walking on the water,
Not of Gennesareth, but Thames!

Francis Thompson

CONSECRATION

Oh God, I offer Thee my heart—
In many a mystic mood, by beauty led,
I give my heart to Thee. But now impart
That sterner grace—to offer Thee my head.

Author unknown

THE RIDDLE OF THE WORLD

The riddle of the world is understood
Only by him who feels that God is good;
As only he can feel who makes his love
The ladder of his faith, and climbs above
On the rounds of his best instincts; draws no line
Between mere human goodness and divine.
But judging God by what in him is best,
With a child's trust leans on a Father's breast.

John Greenleaf Whittier
181

FAITH

There is no unbelief;
Whoever plants a seed beneath the sod
And waits to see it push away the clod,
   He trusts in God.

Whoever says when clouds are in the sky,
"Be patient, heart, light breaketh by and by,"
   Trusts the Most High.

Whoever sees, 'neath fields of winter snow,
The silent harvest of the future grow,
   God's power must know.

Whoever lies down on his couch to sleep,
Content to lock each sense in slumber deep,
   Knows God will keep.

Whoever says, "To-morrow," "The Unknown,"
"The Future," trusts that power alone
   He dares disown.

There is no unbelief;
And day by day and night, unconsciously,
The heart lives by that faith the lips deny,
   God knoweth why.

                   Edward Bulwer-Lytton

CANDLE AND BOOK

One tiny golden upward-pointing flame—
The truth alive forever in men's hearts;
One Holy Book—silent, but thousand-tongued:
Godward we go with candle and with book,
Needing no other symbols of His love.

                   Nina Willis Walter

JUST FOR TODAY

Lord, for to-morrow and its needs,
 I do not pray:
Keep me, my God, from stain of sin,
 Just for to-day;
Let me no wrong or idle word
 Unthinking say:
Set Thou a seal upon my lips,
 Just for to-day.

Let me both diligently work,
 And duly pray;
Let me be kind in word and deed,
 Just for to-day;
Let me in season, Lord, be grave,
 In season, gay;
Let me be faithful to Thy grace,
 Just for to-day.

In pain and sorrow's cleansing fires,
 Brief be my stay;
Oh, bid me if to-day I die,
 Come home to-day;
So, for to-morrow and its needs,
 I do not pray;
But keep me, guide me, love me, Lord,
 Just for to-day.

Sybil F. Partridge

DAY BY DAY

"Day by day," the promise reads;
 Daily strength for daily needs.

Stephen F. Winward

183

AS THY DAYS SO SHALL THY STRENGTH BE

God broke the years to hours and days,
That hour by hour
And day by day,
Just going on a little way,
We might be able all along
To keep quite strong.
Should all the weights of life
Be laid across our shoulders,
And the future, rife
With woe and struggle,
Meet us face to face
At just one place,
We could not go;
Our feet would stop. And so
God lays a little on us every day,
And never, I believe, on all the way,
Will burdens bear so deep,
Or pathways lie so steep,
But we can go, if by God's power
We only bear the burden of the hour.

Georgianu Holmes (George Klingle)

"WITH WHOM IS NO VARIABLENESS, NEITHER SHADOW OF TURNING"

It fortifies my soul to know
That, though I perish, truth is so:
That, howsoe'er I stray and range,
Whate'er I do, Thou dost not change.
I steadier step when I recall
That, if I slip, Thou dost not fall.

Arthur Hugh Clough

184

THE ONE HUNDRED AND TWENTY-FIRST PSALM

I will lift up mine eyes unto the hills:
    from whence cometh my help.
My help cometh from the Lord:
    which made heaven and earth.
He will not suffer thy foot to be moved:
    he that keepeth thee will not slumber.
Behold, he that keepeth Israel
    shall neither slumber nor sleep.
The Lord is thy keeper:
    the Lord is thy shade,
        upon thy right hand.
The sun shall not smite thee by day;
    nor the moon by night.
The Lord shall preserve thee from all evil:
    he shall preserve thy soul.
The Lord shall preserve thy going out,
    and thy coming in:
        from this time forth and even for evermore.

LIGHT SHINING OUT OF DARKNESS

God moves in a mysterious way,
    His wonders to perform;
He plants his footsteps in the sea,
    And rides upon the storm.

Deep in unfathomable mines
    Of never failing skill,
He treasures up his bright designs,
    And works his sovereign will.

Ye fearful saints, fresh courage take;
    The clouds ye so much dread
Are big with mercy, and shall break
    In blessings on your head.

Judge not the Lord by feeble sense,
    But trust him for his grace;
Behind a frowning providence,
    He hides a smiling face.

His purposes will ripen fast,
    Unfolding every hour:
The bud may have a bitter taste,
    But sweet will be the flower.

Blind unbelief is sure to err,
    And scan his work in vain;
God is his own interpreter,
    And he will make it plain.

William Cowper

TUNE THOU MY HARP

Tune Thou my harp;
There is not, Lord, could never be,
The skill in me.

Tune Thou my harp,
That it may play Thy melody,
Thy harmony.

Tune Thou my harp;
O Spirit, breathe Thy thought through me,
As pleaseth Thee.

Amy Carmichael

18. *Hope for Tomorrow*

BIDE A WEE!

Though the times be dark and dreary,
Though the way be long,
Keep your spirits bright and cheery—
—"Bide a wee, and dinna weary!"
 Is a heartsome song.

John Oxenham

HOPE

I shall wear laughter on my lips
Though in my heart is pain—
God's sun is always brightest after rain.

I shall go singing down my little way
Though in my breast the dull ache grows—
The song birds come again after the snows.

I shall walk eager still for what Life holds
Although it seems the hard road will not end—
One never knows the beauty round the bend!

Anna Blake Mezquida

THE TIDE WILL WIN

On the far reef the breakers
    Recoil in shattered foam,
While still the sea behind them
    Urges its forces home;
Its song of triumph surges
    O'er all the thunderous din,
The wave may break in failure,
    But the tide is sure to win!

The reef is strong and cruel;
    Upon its jagged wall
One wave, a score, a hundred,
    Broken and beaten fall;
Yet in defeat they conquer,
    The sea comes flooding in,
Wave upon wave is routed,
    But the tide is sure to win.

O mighty sea! thy message
    In clanging spray is cast;
Within God's plan of progress
    It matters not at last
How wide the shores of evil,
    How strong the reefs of sin,
The wave may be defeated,
    But the tide is sure to win!

Priscilla Leonard

FROM *THE BATTLE-FIELD*

Truth, crushed to earth, shall rise again;
    The eternal years of God are hers;
But Error, wounded, writhes with pain
    And dies among his worshipers.

William Cullen Bryant

188

HOPE

Great God of Hope, how green Thy trees,
  How calm each several star.
Renew us; make us fresh as these,
  Calm as those are.

For what can dim his hope who sees,
  Though faintly and afar,
The power that kindles green in trees,
  And light in star?

Amy Carmichael

SAY NOT THE STRUGGLE NOUGHT AVAILETH

Say not the struggle nought availeth,
  The labour and the wounds are vain,
The enemy faints not, nor faileth.
  And as things have been they remain.

If hopes were dupes, fears may be liars;
  It may be, in yon smoke conceal'd,
Your comrades chase e'en now the fliers,
  And, but for you, possess the field.

For while the tired waves, vainly breaking,
Seem here no painful inch to gain,
Far back, through creeks and inlets making,
  Comes silent, flooding in, the main.

And not by eastern windows only,
  When daylight comes, comes in the light;
In front the sun climbs slow, how slowly!
  But westward, look, the land is bright!

Arthur Hugh Clough

FROM *AT THE WORST*

Evil is here? That's work for us to do.
The Old is dying? Let's beget the New.
And Death awaits us? Rest is but our due.

Israel Zangwill

OBLIQUE

O often have I prayed, and thought
An answer from the skies would come;
Yet heaven would be deaf and dumb;
The firmament no answer brought.
But then in glad surprise I found
My comfort coming from the ground.

Sometimes I have besought the great
To lend their aid that I might bring
Life's flower into blossoming.
I waited; and they let me wait.
But in my need a humble friend
Brought all my trouble to an end.

In night, in solitude I groped
Another's sympathy to find,—
Till to the dark I was resigned,
Thinking that I had vainly hoped.
But, come from realms to me unknown,
I felt love's hand upon my own.

The flight of angels never seems
To be direct. We look before.
But a surprise they have in store:
Not here, but there, the glory streams.
To tell their course in vain we strive;
We only know they shall arrive.

Archibald Rutledge

GOD DOES DO SUCH WONDERFUL THINGS!

God does do such wonderful things!
How can we doubt He'll see us through?
He has proved Himself through a million springs,
Yet still we wonder: "What shall we do?"
The world is black with war and woe—
But look where the pussy willows grow,
And hear the songs and see the wings . . .
God does do such wonderful things!

Angela Morgan

FROM *IN MEMORIAM*

O yet we trust that somehow good
   Will be the final goal of ill,
   To pangs of nature, sins of will,
Defects of doubt, and taints of blood;

That nothing walks with aimless feet,
   That not one life shall be destroy'd,
   Or cast as rubbish to the void,
When God hath made the pile complete;

That not a worm is cloven in vain;
   That not a moth with vain desire
   Is shrivel'd in a fruitless fire,
Or but subserves another's gain.

Behold, we know not anything;
   I can but trust that good shall fall
   At last—far off—at last, to all,
And every winter change to spring.

Alfred Tennyson

191

WHEN NIGHT IS ALMOST DONE

When night is almost done,
And sunrise grows so near
That we can touch the spaces,
It's time to smoothe the hair

And get the dimples ready,
And wonder we could care
For that old faded midnight
That frightened but an hour.

Emily Dickinson

THERE'S A LIGHT UPON THE MOUNTAINS

There's a light upon the mountains,
 And the day is at the spring,
When our eyes shall see the beauty
 And the glory of the King:
Weary was our heart with waiting,
 And the night-watch seemed so long,
But His triumph-day is breaking,
 And we hail it with a song.

In the fading of the starlight
 We may see the coming morn;
And the lights of men are paling
 In the splendors of the dawn;
For the eastern skies are glowing
 As with light of hidden fire,
And the hearts of men are stirring
 With the throbs of deep desire.

There's a hush of expectation
　And a quiet in the air,
And the breath of God is moving
　In the fervent breath of prayer;
For the suffering, dying Jesus
　Is the Christ upon the throne,
And the travail of our spirit
　Is the travail of His own.

He is breaking down the barriers,
　He is casting up the way;
He is calling for His angels
　To build up the gates of day:
But His angels here are human,
　Not the shining hosts above;
For the drum-beats of His army
　Are the heart-beats of our love.

Hark! we hear a distant music,
　And it comes with fuller swell;
'Tis the triumph-song of Jesus,
　Of our King, Immanuel!
Go ye forth with joy to meet Him!
　And, my soul, be swift to bring
All thy sweetest and thy dearest
　For the triumph of our King!

Henry Burton

FROM *TALES OF A WAYSIDE INN*

The dawn is not distant,
Nor is the night starless;
Love is eternal!
God is still God, and
His faith shall not fail us;
Christ is eternal!

Henry Wadsworth Longfellow

THE KING'S HIGHWAY

A wonderful way is the King's Highway;
It runs through the nightland up to the Day;
From the wonderful WAS, by the wonderful IS,
To the still more wonderful IS TO BE
—Runs the King's Highway.

John Masefield

JESUS RETURN

Return, dear Lord, to those who look
  With eager eyes that yearn
For Thee among the garden flowers;
After the dark and lonely hours,
  As morning light return.

Return to those who wander far,
  With lamps that dimly burn,
Along the troubled road of thought,
Where doubt and conflict come unsought,—
  With inward joy return.

Return to those on whom the yoke
  Of life is hard and stern;
Renew the hope within their breast,
Draw them to Thee and give them rest:
  O Friend of Man, return.

Return to this war-weary world,
  And help us all to learn
Thy secret of victorious life,
The love that triumphs over strife,—
  O Prince of Peace, return.

Jesus, we ask not now that day
  When all men shall discern
Thy coming with the angelic host;

Today, to all who need Thee most,
In silent ways, return!

Henry van Dyke

CAPTAIN OF THE YEARS

I watched the Captains
A-riding, riding
Down the years;
The men of mystic grip
Of soul, a-riding
Between a hedge of spears.

I saw their banners
A-floating, floating
Over all,
Till each of them had passed,
And Christ came riding
A donkey lean and small.

I watched the Captains
A-turning, staring,
Proud and set,
At Christ a-riding there—
So calmly riding
The Road men can't forget.

I watched the Captains
Dismounting, waiting—
None now led—
The Captains bowing low!
The Caesars waiting!
While Christ rode on ahead.

Arthur R. Macdougall, Jr.

FROM *THE FORTY-SECOND PSALM*

As the hart panteth after the water brooks,
  so panteth my soul after thee, O God.
My soul thirsteth for God, for the living God:
  when shall I come and appear before God?
My tears have been my meat day and night;
  while they continually say unto me,
    Where is thy God?
When I remember these things,
  I pour out my soul in me;
    for I had gone with the multitude,
      I went with them to the house of God;
  with the voice of joy and praise,
    with a multitude that kept holyday.
Why art thou cast down, O my soul,
  and why art thou disquieted in me?
    hope thou in God . . .
Deep calleth unto deep at the noise of thy waterspouts:
  all thy waves and thy billows are gone over me.
Yet the Lord will command his loving-kindness
  in the daytime,
    and in the night his song shall be with me,
      and my prayer unto the God of my life.

FROM *IN MEMORIAM*

The man, that with me trod
  This planet, was a noble type
  Appearing ere the times were ripe,
That friend of mine who lives in God,

That God, which ever lives and loves,
  One God, one law, one element,
  And one far-off divine event,
To which the whole creation moves.

Alfred Tennyson

FROM *RABBI BEN EZRA*

Grow old along with me!
The best is yet to be,
The last of life, for which the first was made:
Our times are in his hand
Who saith, "A whole I planned,
Youth shows but half; trust God: see all, nor be afraid!"

Robert Browning

EVENSONG

Though the day be never so long
At last it ringeth to evensong.

George Tankervil

DO WE NOT HEAR THY FOOTFALL?

Do we not hear Thy footfall, O Belovèd,
    Among the stars on many a moonless night?
Do we not catch the whisper of Thy coming
    On winds of dawn, and often in the light
Of noontide and of sunset almost see Thee?
    Look up through shining air
And long to see Thee, O Belovèd, long to see Thee,
    And wonder that Thou art not standing there?

And we shall hear Thy footfall, O Belovèd,
    And starry ways will open, and the night
Will call her candles from their distant stations,
    And winds shall sing Thee, noon, and mingled light
Of rose-red evening thrill with lovely welcome;
    And we, caught up in air,
Shall see Thee, O Belovèd, we shall see Thee,
    In hush of adoration see Thee there.

Amy Carmichael
197

THE FORTY-SIXTH PSALM

God is our refuge and strength:
  a very present help in trouble.
Therefore will not we fear,
    though the earth be removed,
      and though the mountains
        be carried into the midst of the sea;
Though the waters thereof roar, and be troubled,
    though the mountains shake with the swelling thereof.
                                                    Selah.

There is a river,
    the streams whereof shall make glad the city of God:
      the holy place of the tabernacles of the most High.
God is in the midst of her:
    she shall not be moved;
      God shall help her, and that right early.
The heathen raged, the kingdoms were moved:
    he uttered his voice, the earth melted.
The Lord of hosts is with us;
    the God of Jacob is our refuge.
                                                    Selah.

Come, behold the works of the Lord,
    what desolations he hath made in the earth.
He maketh wars to cease unto the end of the earth:
    he breaketh the bow, and cutteth the spear in sunder;
      he burneth the chariot in the fire.
Be still, and know that I am God:
    I will be exalted among the heathen,
      I will be exalted in the earth.
The Lord of hosts is with us;
    the God of Jacob is our refuge.
                                                    Selah.

19. *The Way of Love*

WHERE TO SEEK LOVE

I thought Love lived in the hot sunshine,
But O he lives in the moony light!
I thought to find Love in the heat of day,
But sweet Love is the comforter of night.

Seek Love in the pity of others' woe,
In the gentle relief of another's care,
In the darkness of night and the winter's snow,
In the naked and outcast, seek Love there.

William Blake

SONNET 116

Let me not to the marriage of true minds
Admit impediments. Love is not love
Which alters when it alteration finds,
Or bends with the remover to remove.
O, no! it is an ever-fixèd mark,
That looks on tempests and is never shaken;
It is the star to every wandering bark,
Whose worth's unknown, although his height be taken.
Love's not Time's fool, though rosy lips and cheeks
Within his bending sickle's compass come;
Love alters not with his brief hours and weeks,
But bears it out even to the edge of doom.
    If this be error and upon me proved,
    I never writ, nor no man ever loved.

William Shakespeare

OUTWITTED

He drew a circle that shut me out—
Heretic, rebel, a thing to flout.
But Love and I had the wit to win:
We drew a circle that took him in!

Edwin Markham

MEDITATION

Holding a beggar's child
    Against my heart,
Through blinding tears I see
    That as I love the tiny, piteous thing,
So God loves me!

Toyohiko Kagawa

FROM THE RIME OF THE ANCIENT MARINER

He prayeth best, who loveth best
All things both great and small;
For the dear God who loveth us,
He made and loveth all.

Samuel Taylor Coleridge

FROM A DEATH IN THE DESERT

For life, with all it yields of joy and woe,
And hope and fear,—believe the aged friend,—
Is just our chance o' the prize of learning love,
How love might be, hath been indeed, and is;
And that we hold thenceforth to the uttermost
Such prize despite the envy of the world,
And, having gained truth, keep truth: that is all.

Robert Browning

THE MASTER-PLAYER

An old, worn harp that had been played
Till all its strings were loose and frayed,
Joy, Hate, and Fear, each one essayed,
To play. But each in turn had found
No sweet responsiveness of sound.

Then Love the Master-Player came
With heaving breast and eyes aflame;
The Harp he took all undismayed,
Smote on its strings, still strange to song,
And brought forth music sweet and strong.

Paul Laurence Dunbar

FOLKS NEED A LOT OF LOVING

Folks need a lot of loving in the morning;
   The day is all ahead, with cares beset—
The cares we know, and those that give no warning;
   For love is God's own antidote for fret.

Folks need a heap of loving at the noontime—
   The battle lull, the moment snatched from strife—
Halfway between the waking and the croontime,
   When bickering and worriment are rife.

Folks hunger so for loving at the nighttime,
   When wearily they take them home to rest—
At slumber song and turning-out-the-light time.
   Of all the times for loving, that's the best.

Folks want a lot of loving every minute—
   The sympathy of others and their smile!
Till life's end, from the moment they begin it,
   Folks need a lot of loving all the while.

Strickland Gillilan

FROM *THE MERCHANT OF VENICE*

The quality of mercy is not strain'd,
It droppeth as the gentle rain from heaven
Upon the place beneath. It is twice bless'd:
It blesseth him that gives and him that takes.
'Tis mightiest in the mightiest: it becomes
The thronéd monarch better than his crown:
His sceptre shows the force of temporal power,
The attribute to awe and majesty,
Wherein doth sit the dread and fear of kings;
But mercy is above this sceptred sway,
It is enthronéd in the hearts of kings,
It is an attribute to God himself;
And earthly power doth then show likest God's,
When mercy seasons justice. Therefore . . .
Though justice be thy plea, consider this—
That in the course of justice none of us
Should see salvation. We do pray for mercy;
And that same prayer doth teach us all to render
The deeds of mercy.

William Shakespeare

BY NIGHT

The tapers in the great God's hall
    Burn ageless, beautiful and white,
But only with the fall of dusk
    Disclose to earth their faithful light.

Earth keeps her lamps of beauty, too,
    Fairer than stars in fields above;
Dark hours of grief and pain reveal
    The undreamed constancy of love.

Philip Jerome Cleveland

202

THE WAY

Who seeks for heaven alone to save his soul,
May keep the path, but will not reach the goal;
While he who walks in love may wander far,
But God will bring him where the Blessed are.

Henry van Dyke

MY DAILY CREED

Let me be a little kinder,
　Let me be a little blinder
To the faults of those about me;
　Let me praise a little more;
Let me be, when I am weary,
　Just a little bit more cheery;
Let me serve a little better
　Those that I am striving for.

Let me be a little braver
　When temptation bids me waver;
Let me strive a little harder
　To be all that I should be;
Let me be a little meeker
　With the brother that is weaker;
Let me think more of my neighbor
　And a little less of me.

Author unknown

THEOLOGY

There is a heaven, for ever, day by day,
The upward longing of my soul doth tell me so.
There is a hell, I'm quite as sure; for pray,
If there were not, where would my neighbours go?

Paul Laurence Dunbar

AT SET OF SUN

If you sit down at set of sun
And count the acts that you have done,
  And, counting, find
One self-denying deed, one word
That eased the heart of him who heard—
  One glance most kind,
That fell like sunshine where it went—
Then you may count that day well spent.

But, if, through all the livelong day,
You've cheered no heart, by yea or nay—
  If, through it all
You've nothing done that you can trace
That brought the sunshine to one face—
  No act most small
That helped some soul and nothing cost—
Then count that day as worse than lost.

George Eliot

LOVE

Though I speak with the tongues of men and of angels,
And have not love,
I am become as sounding brass, or a tinkling cymbal.
And though I have the gift of prophecy,
And understand all mysteries, and all knowledge;
And though I have all faith, so that I could remove mountains,
And have not love,
I am nothing.
And though I bestow all my goods to feed the poor,
And though I give my body to be burned,
And have not love,
It profiteth me nothing.
  Love suffereth long, and is kind;
Love envieth not;

Love vaunteth not itself, is not puffed up,
Doth not behave itself unseemly,
Seeketh not its own,
Is not easily provoked,
Thinketh no evil;
Rejoiceth not in iniquity, but rejoiceth in the truth;
Beareth all things,
Believeth all things,
Hopeth all things,
Endureth all things.
Love never faileth:
But whether there be prophecies, they shall fail;
Whether there be tongues, they shall cease;
Whether there be knowledge, it shall vanish away.
For we know in part, and we prophesy in part.
But when that which is perfect is come,
That which is in part shall be done away.
When I was a child, I spake as a child,
I understood as a child, I thought as a child:
But when I became a man, I put away childish things.
For now we see through a glass, darkly;
But then face to face:
Now I know in part;
But then shall I know even as also I am known.
And now abideth faith, hope, love, these three;
But the greatest of these is love.

Paul (I Corinthians 13)

PHILOSOPHERS HAVE MEASURED MOUNTAINS

Philosophers have measured mountains,
Fathomed the depths of seas, of fates, and kings,
Walked with a staff to heav'n, and traced fountains:
But there are two vast, spacious things,
The which to measure it doth more behove:
Yet few there are that found them; Sin and Love.

George Herbert

205

ABOU BEN ADHEM

Abou Ben Adhem (may his tribe increase)
Awoke one night from a deep dream of peace,
And saw—within the moonlight in his room,
Making it rich and like a lily in bloom—
An angel, writing in a book of gold.
Exceeding peace had made Ben Adhem bold,
And to the presence in the room he said,
'What writest thou?'—The vision raised its head,
And, with a look made of all sweet accord,
Answered, 'The names of those who love the Lord.'
'And is mine one?' said Abou. 'Nay, not so,'
Replied the angel. Abou spoke more low,
But cheerly still, and said, 'I pray thee, then,
Write me as one that loves his fellow men.'

The angel wrote and vanished. The next night
It came again with a great wakening light,
And showed the names whom love of God had blessed,
And lo! Ben Adhem's name led all the rest.

James Henry Leigh Hunt

WE ARE GOD'S CHOSEN FEW

We are God's chosen few,
All others will be damned;
There is no place in heaven for you,
We can't have heaven crammed!

Jonathan Swift

BY GENTLE LOVE

May we and all who bear thy name
By gentle love thy cross proclaim,
The gift of peace on earth secure,
And for thy Truth the world endure.

Author unknown

20. Joy and Peace Within

THE PLACE OF PEACE

At the heart of the cyclone tearing the sky
And flinging the clouds and the towers by,
Is a place of central calm;
So here in the roar of mortal things,
I have a place where my spirit sings,
In the hollow of God's palm.

Edwin Markham

REFLECTIONS

Stars lie broken on a lake
Whenever passing breezes make
    The wavelets leap;
But when the lake is still, the sky
Gives moon and stars that they may lie
    On that calm deep.

If, like the lake that has the boon
Of cradling the little moon
    Above the hill,
I want the Infinite to be
Reflected undisturbed in me,
    I must be still.

Edna Becker

JOY AND PEACE IN BELIEVING

Sometimes a light surprises
  The Christian while he sings;
It is the Lord who rises
  With healing in his wings:
When comforts are declining,
  He grants the soul again
A season of clear shining
  To cheer it after rain.

In holy contemplation,
  We sweetly then pursue
The theme of God's salvation,
  And find it ever new:
Set free from present sorrow,
  We cheerfully can say,
E'en let th' unknown tomorrow
  Bring with it what it may.

It can bring with it nothing
  But he will bear us thro';
Who gives the lilies clothing
  Will clothe his people too:
Beneath the spreading heavens,
  No creature but is fed;
And he who feeds the ravens
  Will give his children bread.

Though vine, nor fig tree neither,
  Their wonted fruit should bear,
Tho' all the fields should wither,
  Nor flocks, nor herds, be there:
Yet God the same abiding,
  His praise shall tune my voice;
For while in him confiding,
  I cannot but rejoice.

William Cowper

SHEER JOY

Oh the sheer joy of it!
    Living with Thee,
God of the universe,
    Lord of a tree,
Maker of mountains,
    Lover of me!

Oh the sheer joy of it!
    Breathing thy air;
Morning is dawning,
    Gone every care,
All the world's singing,
    "God's everywhere."

Oh the sheer joy of it!
    Walking with Thee,
Out on the hilltop,
    Down by the sea,
Life is so wonderful,
    Life is so free.

Oh the sheer joy of it!
    Working with God,
Running His errands,
    Waiting His nod,
Building His heaven,
    On common sod.

Oh the sheer joy of it!
    Ever to be
Living in glory,
    Living with Thee,
Lord of tomorrow,
    Lover of me!

Ralph Spaulding Cushman

209

CHRIST'S BONDSERVANT

Make me a captive, Lord,
  And then I shall be free;
Force me to render up my sword,
  And I shall conqueror be.
I sink in life's alarms
  When by myself I stand;
Imprison me within Thine arms,
  And strong shall be my hand.

My heart is weak and poor
  Until it master find;
It has no spring of action sure—
  It varies with the wind:
It cannot freely move
  Till Thou hast wrought its chain;
Enslave it with Thy matchless love,
  And deathless it shall reign.

My power is faint and low
  Till I have learned to serve:
It wants the needed fire to glow,
  It wants the breeze to nerve;
It cannot drive the world
  Until itself be driven;
Its flag can only be unfurled
  When Thou shalt breathe from heaven.

My will is not my own
  Till Thou hast made it Thine;
If it would reach a monarch's throne
  It must its crown resign:
It only stands unbent
  Amid the clashing strife,
When on Thy bosom it has leant
  And found in Thee its life.

George Matheson

BLIND BUT HAPPY

O what a happy soul am I!
 Although I cannot see,
I am resolved that in this world
 Contented I will be;
How many blessings I enjoy
 That other people don't!
To weep and sigh because I'm blind,
 I cannot, and I won't.

   Fanny Crosby (written at the age of eight)

HE WALKS AT PEACE

But there is one, they say,
So sure of life,
That the claw of the tiger,
The horn of the buffalo,
And the point of the sword
Find him not.
And why?
Because he walks at peace with life
And death.

     Tao Tê Ching

FROM *THE CHRISTIAN SOLDIER*

Peace does not mean the end of all our striving,
 Joy does not mean the drying of our tears,
Peace is the power that comes to souls arriving
 Up to the light where God Himself appears.

Joy is the wine that God is ever pouring
 Into the hearts of those who strive with Him,

Light'ning their eyes to vision and adoring,
　Strength'ning their arms to warfare glad and grim.

G. A. Studdert-Kennedy

THERE'S A WIDENESS IN GOD'S MERCY

There's a wideness in God's mercy,
Like the wideness of the sea;
There's a kindness in his justice,
Which is more than liberty.

There is no place where earth's sorrows
Are more felt than up in heaven;
There is no place where earth's failings
Have such kindly judgment given.

For the love of God is broader
Than the measure of man's mind;
And the heart of the Eternal
Is most wonderfully kind.

If our love were but more simple,
We should take him at his word;
And our lives would be all sunshine
In the sweetness of our Lord.

Frederick W. Faber

CALM SOUL OF ALL THINGS

Calm soul of all things! be it mine
　To feel amid the city's jar,
That there abides a peace of thine
　Man did not make and cannot mar!

The will to neither strive nor cry,
　The power to feel with others give!

> Calm, calm me more! nor let me die
> Before I have begun to live!
>
> *Matthew Arnold*

FROM *THE EVERLASTING MERCY*

I did not think, I did not strive,
The deep peace burnt my me alive;
The bolted door had broken in,
I knew that I had done with sin.
I knew that Christ had given me birth
To brother all the souls on earth,
And every bird and every beast
Should share the crumbs broke at the feast.

O glory of the lighted mind.
How dead I'd been, how dumb, how blind.
The station brook, to my new eyes,
Was babbling out of Paradise,
The waters rushing from the rain
Were singing Christ has risen again.
I thought all earthly creatures knelt
From rapture of the joy I felt.

John Masefield

TODAY

Build a little fence of trust
    Around today;
Fill the space with loving deeds,
    And therein stay.
Look not through the sheltering bars
    Upon tomorrow;
God will help thee bear what comes
    Of joy or sorrow.

Mary Frances Butts

213

NOW AND THEN

There were hours when life was bitter
    With the anguish of defeat,
When strange it seemed that anything
    Had ever tasted sweet.
And we scarce knew how to bear it,
    But One came o'er the wave,
And the peace He gave us with a word
    Then made us strong and brave.

There are hours when work is pressing,
    Just little homely work
That must be done, that we must do,
    That it were shame to shirk,
And in those hours full often,
    To crown the petty cares,
Has fallen upon the house a gleam
    Of God's Heaven unawares.

So, for our hallowed hours
    We find them, where our Lord
Has called us into service meet
    For blessing and reward;
They are sometimes in the closet,
    They are often in the mart,
And the Lord can make them anywhere,
    His "desert place apart."

Margaret E. Sangster

PERFECT PEACE

Thou wilt keep him in perfect peace,
    whose mind is stayed on thee;
        because he trusteth in thee.

Isaiah the Prophet (Isaiah 26:3)

DEAR LORD AND FATHER OF MANKIND

Dear Lord and Father of mankind!
　Forgive our foolish ways!
Reclothe us in our rightful mind,
In purer lives Thy service find,
　In deeper reverence, praise.

In simple trust like theirs who heard,
　Beside the Syrian sea,
The gracious calling of the Lord,
Let us, like them, without a word,
　Rise up and follow Thee.

O Sabbath rest by Galilee!
　O calm of hills above,
Where Jesus knelt to share with Thee
The silence of eternity
　Interpreted by love!

With that deep hush subduing all
　Our words and works that drown
The tender whisper of Thy call,
As noiseless let Thy blessing fall
　As fell Thy manna down.

Drop Thy still dews of quietness,
　Till all our strivings cease;
Take from our souls the strain and stress,
And let our ordered lives confess
　The beauty of Thy peace.

Breathe through the heats of our desire
　Thy coolness and Thy balm;
Let sense be dumb, let flesh retire;
Speak through the earthquake, wind and fire,
　O still small voice of calm!

John Greenleaf Whittier

THE EVENING STAR

Lord, art Thou wrapped in cloud,
  That prayer should not pass through?
But heart that knows Thee sings aloud,
  Beyond the grey, the blue;
Look up, look up to the hills afar,
And see in clearness the Evening Star.

Should misty weather try
  The temper of the soul,
Come, Lord, and purge and fortify,
  And let Thy hands make whole,
Till we look up to the hills afar,
And see in clearness the Evening Star.

Oh, never twilight dim
  But candles bright are lit,
And then the heavenly vesper hymn—
  The peace of God in it,
As we look up to the hills afar,
And see in clearness the Evening Star.

Amy Carmichael

FROM *HOW CAN I KEEP FROM SINGING?*

What though my joys and comforts die?
  The Lord my Saviour liveth;
What though the darkness gather round?
  Songs in the night He giveth;
No storm can shake my inmost calm,
  While to that refuge clinging;
Since Christ is Lord of heaven and earth,
  How can I keep from singing?

Robert Lowry

21. Divine Guidance

A HYMN
AFTER READING "LEAD, KINDLY LIGHT"

Lead gently, Lord, and slow,
　For oh, my steps are weak,
And ever as I go,
　Some soothing sentence speak;

That I may turn my face
　Through doubt's obscurity
Toward thine abiding-place,
　Ev'n tho' I cannot see.

For lo, the way is dark;
　Through mist and cloud I grope,
Save for that fitful spark,
　The little flame of hope.

Lead gently, Lord, and slow,
　For fear that I may fall;
I know not where to go
　Unless I hear thy call.

My fainting soul doth yearn
　For thy green hills afar;
So let thy mercy burn—
　My greater, guiding star!

Paul Laurence Dunbar

VOYAGERS

O Maker of the Mighty Deep
   Whereon our vessels fare,
Above our life's adventure keep
   Thy faithful watch and care.
In Thee we trust, whate'er befall;
Thy sea is great, our boats are small.

We know not where the secret tides
   Will help us or delay,
Nor where the lurking tempest hides,
   Nor where the fogs are gray.
We trust in Thee, whate'er befall;
Thy sea is great, our boats are small.

When outward bound we boldly sail
   And leave the friendly shore,
Let not our hearts of courage fail
   Before the voyage is o'er.
We trust in Thee, whate'er befall;
Thy sea is great, our boats are small.

When homeward bound we gladly turn,
   O bring us safely there,
Where harbour-lights of friendship burn
   And peace is in the air.
We trust in Thee, whate'er befall;
Thy sea is great, our boats are small.

Beyond the circle of the sea,
   When voyaging is past,
We seek our final port in Thee;
   O bring us home at last.
In Thee we trust, whate'er befall;
Thy sea is great, our boats are small.

Henry van Dyke

THY WAY, NOT MINE

Thy way, not mine, O Lord,
　However dark it be!
Lead me byThine own hand,
　Choose out the path for me.

Smooth let it be or rough,
　It will be still the best;
Winding or straight, it leads
　Right onward to Thy rest.

I dare not choose my lot;
　I would not, if I might;
Choose Thou for me, my God;
　So shall I walk aright.

The kingdom that I seek
　Is Thine; so let the way
That leads to it be Thine;
　Else I must surely stray.

Take Thou my cup, and it
　With joy or sorrow fill,
As best to Thee may seem;
　Choose Thou my good and ill;

Choose Thou for me my friends,
　My sickness or my health;
Choose Thou my cares for me,
　My poverty or wealth.

Not mine, not mine the choice,
　In things or great or small;
Be Thou my guide, my strength,
　My wisdom, and my all!

Horatius Bonar

FROM *SAINT PATRICK'S BREASTPLATE*

I bind unto myself to-day
The power of God to hold and lead,
His eye to watch, His might to stay,
His ear to hearken to my need,
The wisdom of my God to teach,
His hand to guide, His shield to ward;
The word of God to give me speech,
His heavenly host to be my guard.

I bind unto myself the name,
The strong name of the Trinity;
By invocation of the same
The Three in One and One in Three,
Of whom all nature hath creation;
Eternal Father, Spirit, Word;
Praise to the Lord of my salvation,
Salvation is of *Christ* the *Lord*.

St. Patrick

TO A WATERFOWL

Whither, midst falling dew,
While glow the heavens with the last steps of day,
Far, through their rosy depths, dost thou pursue
Thy solitary way?

Vainly the fowler's eye
Might mark thy distant flight to do thee wrong,
As, darkly seen against the crimson sky,
Thy figure floats along.

Seek'st thou the plashy brink
Of weedy lake, or marge of river wide,
Or where the rocking billows rise and sink
On the chafed ocean-side?

There is a Power whose care
Teaches thy way along that pathless coast—
The desert and illimitable air—
    Lone wandering, but not lost.

All day thy wings have fanned,
At that far height, the cold, thin atmosphere,
Yet stoop not, weary, to the welcome land,
    Though the dark night is near.

And soon that toil shall end;
Soon shalt thou find a summer home, and rest,
And scream among thy fellows; reeds shall bend,
    Soon, o'er thy sheltered nest.

Thou'rt gone, the abyss of heaven
Hath swallowed up thy form; yet, on my heart
Deeply has sunk the lesson thou hast given,
    And shall not soon depart.

He who, from zone to zone,
Guides through the boundless sky thy certain flight,
In the long way that I must tread alone,
    Will lead my steps aright.

               William Cullen Bryant

From *NOT KNOWING*

I know not what shall befall me: God hangs a mist o'er my eyes;
And thus, each step of my onward path,
    He makes new scenes arise,
And every joy He sends to me comes like a sweet surprise.

        *   *   *

So I go on not knowing,—I would not if I might;
I would rather walk in the dark with God

than go alone in the light;
I would rather walk with Him by faith than walk alone by sight.

Mary Gardiner Brainard

BE STILL, MY SOUL

Be still, my soul: the Lord is on thy side;
   Bear patiently the cross of grief or pain;
Leave to thy God to order and provide;
   In every change he faithful will remain.
Be still, my soul: thy best, thy heavenly Friend
Through thorny ways leads to a joyful end.

Be still, my soul: thy God doth undertake
   To guide the future as he has the past.
Thy hope, thy confidence let nothing shake;
   All now mysterious shall be bright at last.
Be still, my soul: the waves and winds still know
His voice who ruled them while he dwelt below.

Katharina von Schlegel
(translated by Jane L. Borthwick)

EVENSONG

The embers of the day are red
Beyond the murky hill.
The kitchen smokes; the bed
In the darkling house is spread:
The great sky darkens overhead,
And the great woods are shrill.
So far have I been led,
Lord, by Thy will:
So far I have followed, Lord, and wondered still.
The breeze from the embalmèd land

Blows sudden towards the shore,
And claps my cottage door.
I hear the signal, Lord—I understand.
The night at Thy command
Comes. I will eat and sleep and will not question more.

Robert Louis Stevenson

WALKING WITH GOD

O for a closer walk with God,
    A calm and heavenly frame,
A light to shine upon the road
    That leads me to the Lamb!

Where is the blessedness I knew
    When first I saw the Lord?
Where is the soul-refreshing view
    Of Jesus and His word?

What peaceful hours I once enjoy'd!
    How sweet their memory still!
But they have left an aching void,
    The world can never fill.

Return, O holy Dove, return,
    Sweet messenger of rest:
I hate the sins that made Thee mourn,
    And drove Thee from my breast.

The dearest idol I have known,
    Whate'er that idol be,
Help me to tear it from Thy throne,
    And worship only Thee.

So shall my walk be close with God,
    Calm and serene my frame;

So purer light shall mark the road
That leads me to the Lamb.

William Cowper

OBEDIENCE

I said, "Let me walk in the fields."
    He said, "No, walk in the town."
I said, "There are no flowers there."
    He said, "No flowers, but a crown."

I said, "But the skies are black;
    There is nothing but noise and din."
And He wept as He sent me back;
    "There is more," He said; "there is sin."

I said, "But the air is thick,
    And fogs are veiling the sun."
He answered, "Yet souls are sick,
    And souls in the dark undone."

I said, "I shall miss the light,
    And friends will miss me, they say."
He answered, "Choose to-night
    If I am to miss you, or they."

I pleaded for time to be given.
    He said, "Is it hard to decide?
It will not seem hard in heaven
    To have followed the steps of your Guide."

I cast one look at the fields,
    Then set my face to the town;
He said, "My child, do you yield?
    Will you leave the flowers for the crown?"

Then into His hand went mine,
    And into my heart came He;
And I walk in a light divine
    The path I had feared to see.

George Macdonald

DISAPPOINTMENT

"Disappointment—His appointment,"
    Change one letter, then I see
That the thwarting of my purpose
    Is God's better choice for me.
His appointment must be blessing,
    Though it may come in disguise,
For the end from the beginning
    Open to His wisdom lies.

"Disappointment—His appointment,"
    Whose? The Lord's, Who loves me best
Understands and knows me fully,
    Who my faith and love would test;
For, like loving earthly parent,
    He rejoices when He knows
That His child accepts, unquestioned,
    All that from His wisdom flows.

"Disappointment—His appointment,"
    "No good thing will He withhold,"
From denials oft we gather
    Treasures of His love untold.
Well He knows each broken purpose
    Leads to fuller, deeper trust,
And the end of all His dealings
    Proves our God is wise and just.

"Disappointment—His appointment,"
    Lord, I take it, then, as such,
Like the clay in hands of potter,
    Yielding wholly to Thy touch,
All my life's plan in Thy moulding,
    Not one single choice be mine;
Let me answer, unrepining—
    Father, "Not my will, but Thine."

Edith Lillian Young

THE PILLAR OF THE CLOUD

Lead, Kindly Light, amid the encircling gloom,
    Lead Thou me on!
The night is dark, and I am far from home—
    Lead Thou me on!
Keep Thou my feet; I do not ask to see
The distant scene,—one step enough for me.

I was not ever thus, nor pray'd that Thou
    Shouldst lead me on.
I lov'd to choose and see my path; but now
    Lead Thou me on!
I lov'd the garish day, and, spite of fears,
Pride rul'd my will: remember not past years.

So long Thy power hath bless'd me, sure it still
    Will lead me on,
O'er moor and fen, o'er crag and torrent, till
    The night is gone;
And with the morn those angel faces smile
Which I have lov'd long since, and lost awhile.

John Henry Newman

THE TWENTY-THIRD PSALM

The Lord is my shepherd;
  I shall not want.
He maketh me to lie down in green pastures:
  he leadeth me beside the still waters.
He restoreth my soul:
  he leadeth me in the paths of righteousness
    for his name's sake.
Yea, though I walk through the valley
  of the shadow of death,
    I will fear no evil:
      for thou art with me;
        thy rod and thy staff they comfort me.
Thou preparest a table before me
  in the presence of mine enemies:
    thou anointest my head with oil;
      my cup runneth over.
Surely goodness and mercy shall follow me
  all the days of my life:
    and I will dwell in the house of the Lord
    for ever.

FROM *AN INVOCATION*

O God, unknown, invisible, secure,
Whose being by dim resemblances we guess,
Who in man's fear and love abidest sure,
Whose power we feel in darkness and confess!

Without Thee nothing is, and Thou art nought
When on Thy substance we gaze curiously:
By Thee impalpable, named Force and Thought,
The solid world still ceases not to be.

Lead Thou me God, Law, Reason, Duty, Life!
All names for Thee alike are vain and hollow—

Lead me, for I will follow without strife;
Or, if I strive, still must I blindly follow.

John Addington Symonds

THE DAY—THE WAY

Not for one single day
Can I discern my way,
    But this I surely know—
Who gives the day
Will show the way,
    So I securely go.

John Oxenham

DIRECT THIS DAY

Lord, I my vows to Thee renew;
Disperse my sins as morning dew:
Guard my first springs of thought and will,
And with Thyself my spirit fill.

Direct, control, suggest this day
All I design, or do, or say;
That all my powers, with all their might,
In Thy sole glory may unite.

Thomas Ken

SILENCE

Let thy soul walk slowly in thee,
    As a saint in heaven unshod,
For to be alone with Silence
    Is to be alone with God.

Samuel Miller Hageman

22. Work, Duty, and Service

THE SWEETEST LIVES

The sweetest lives are those to duty wed,
  Whose deeds, both great and small,
Are close-knit strands of unbroken thread
  Where love ennobles all.
The world may sound no trumpets, ring no bells;
  The book of life the shining record tells.

The love shall chant its own beatitudes
After its own life working. A child's kiss
Set on thy sighing lips shall make thee glad;
A sick man helped by thee shall make thee strong;
Thou shalt be served thyself by every sense
Of service which thou renderest.

Elizabeth Barrett Browning

I WOULD BE TRUE

I would be true, for there are those who trust me;
I would be pure, for there are those who care;
I would be strong, for there is much to suffer;
I would be brave, for there is much to dare.
I would be friend of all—the foe, the friendless;
I would be giving, and forget the gift,
I would be humble, for I know my weakness,
I would look up, and love, and laugh and lift.

Howard Arnold Walter

WORKING WITH GOD

FROM "STRADIVARIUS"

God be praised,
Antonio Stradivari has an eye
That winces at false work and loves the true . . .
And for my fame—when any master holds
'Twixt chin and hand a violin of mine,
He will be glad that Stradivari lived,
Made violins, and made them of the best . . .

I say not God Himself can make man's best
Without best men to help Him . . .
          'Tis God gives skill,
But not without men's hands: He could not make
Antonio Stradivari's violins
Without Antonio.

                                        George Eliot

ON HIS BLINDNESS

When I consider how my light is spent,
  Ere half my days, in this dark world and wide,
  And that one talent which is death to hide
  Lodged with me useless, though my soul more bent
To serve therewith my Maker, and present
  My true account, less He returning chide,
  "Doth God exact day-labor, light denied?"
  I fondly ask. But Patience to prevent
That murmur, soon replies, "God doth not need
  Either man's work or his own gifts. Who best
  Bear his mild yoke, they serve him best. His state
Is kingly: thousands at his bidding speed
  And post o'er land and ocean without rest;
  They also serve who only stand and wait."

                                        John Milton

O TO BE UP AND DOING

O to be up and doing, O
Unfearing and unshamed to go
In all the uproar and the press
About my human business! . . .
For still the Lord is Lord of might:
In deeds, in deeds he takes delight;
The plough, the spear, the laden barks,
The field, the founded city, marks;
He marks the smiler of the streets,
The singers upon garden seats; . . .
Those he approves that ply the trade,
That rock the child, that wed the maid,
That with weak virtues, weaker hands,
Sow gladness on the peopled lands,
And still with laughter, song and shout,
Spin the great wheel of earth about.

Robert Louis Stevenson

A TEACHER'S PRAYER

Lord, speak to me that I may speak
    In living echoes of thy tone;
As thou hast sought, so let me seek
    Thy erring children lost and lone.

O teach me, Lord, that I may teach
    The precious truths thou dost impart,
And wing my words, that they may reach
    The hidden depths of many a heart.

O fill me with thy fulness, Lord,
    Until my very heart o'erflow
In kindling thought and glowing word
    Thy love to tell, thy praise to show.

Frances Ridley Havergal

231

WORK

Let me but do my work from day to day
  In field or forest, at the desk or loom,
  In roaring market-place or tranquil room;
Let me but find it in my heart to say,
When vagrant wishes beckon me astray,
  "This is my work; my blessing, not my doom;
  Of all who live, I am the one by whom
This work can best be done in the right way."

Then shall I see it not too great, nor small,
  To suit my spirit and to prove my powers;
  Then shall I cheerful greet the labouring hours,
And cheerful turn, when the long shadows fall
At eventide, to play and love and rest,
Because I know for me my work is best.

Henry van Dyke

LORD OF ALL POTS AND PANS AND THINGS

Lord of all pots and pans and things, since I've not time to be
A saint by doing lovely things or watching late with Thee,
Or dreaming in the dawn light or storming Heaven's gates,
Make me a saint by getting meals and washing up the plates.

Although I must have Martha's hands, I have a Mary mind
And when I black the boots and shoes, Thy sandals, Lord, I find.
I think of how they trod the earth, what time I scrub the floor;
Accept this meditation, Lord, I haven't time for more.

Warm all the kitchen with Thy love, and light it with Thy peace.
Forgive me all my worrying and make my grumbling cease.
Thou who didst love to give men food, in room or by the sea,
Accept this service that I do, I do it unto Thee.

This poem has been attributed to various authors but appears to be re-worked from "The Divine Office of the Kitchen" by Cecily Hallack.

232

FROM *VOLUNTARIES*

So nigh is grandeur to our dust,
   So near is God to man;
When Duty whispers low, "Thou must,"
   The youth replies, "I can."

                   Ralph Waldo Emerson

THE BRIDGE BUILDER

An old man going a lone highway
Came at the evening, cold and gray,
To a chasm vast and wide and steep,
With waters rolling cold and deep.
The old man crossed in the twilight dim,
The sullen stream had no fears for him;
But he turned when safe on the other side,
And built a bridge to span the tide.

"Old man," said a fellow pilgrim near,
"You are wasting your strength with building here.
Your journey will end with the ending day,
You never again will pass this way.
You've crossed the chasm, deep and wide,
Why build you this bridge at eventide?"

The builder lifted his old gray head.
"Good friend, in the path I have come," he said,
"There followeth after me today
A youth whose feet must pass this way.
The chasm that was as nought to me
To that fair-haired youth may a pitfall be;
He, too, must cross in the twilight dim—
Good friend, I am building this bridge for him."

                   Will Allen Dromgoole

TRUE REST

Rest is not quitting
The busy career;
Rest is the fitting
Of self to one's sphere.

'Tis the brook's motion
Clear without strife,
Fleeting to ocean,
After this life.

'Tis loving and serving,
The highest and best;
'Tis onward, unswerving,
And this is true rest.

Johann Wolfgang von Goethe

THE JOB THAT'S CRYING TO BE DONE

There's not a pair of legs so thin, there's not a head so thick,
There's not a hand so weak and white, nor yet a heart so sick,
But it can find some needful job that's crying to be done
For the glory of the Garden glorifieth every one.

Rudyard Kipling

WE CANNOT KINDLE

We cannot kindle when we will
The fire which in the heart resides,
The spirit bloweth and is still,
In mystery our soul abides:
But tasks, in hours of insight will'd,
May be through hours of gloom fulfilled.

Matthew Arnold

234

SERVICE

O Master, let me walk with Thee
In lowly paths of service free;
Tell me Thy secret; help me bear
The strain of toil, the fret of care.

Help me the slow of heart to move
By some clear, winning word of love;
Teach me the wayward feet to stay,
And guide them in the homeward way.

Teach me Thy patience; still with Thee
In closer, dearer company,
In work that keeps faith sweet and strong,
In trust that triumphs over wrong;

In hope that sends a shining ray
Far down the future's broadening way;
In peace that only Thou canst give,—
With Thee, O Master, let me live.

Washington Gladden

YOUR PLACE

Is your place a small place?
Tend it with care!—
He set you there.

Is your place a large place?
Guard it with care!—
He set you there.

Whate'er your place, it is
Not yours alone, but His
Who set you there.

John Oxenham

235

LEND A HAND

I am only one,
But still I am one.
I cannot do everything,
But still I can do something;
And because I cannot do everything
I will not refuse to do the something
        that I can do.

Edward Everett Hale

TEACH US TO SERVE THEE, LORD

Teach us, good Lord, to serve Thee as Thou deservest:
To give and not to count the cost;
To fight and not to heed the wounds;
To toil and not to seek for rest;
To labor and not ask for any reward
        save that of knowing that we do Thy will. Amen.

St. Ignatius of Loyola

SEND ME

Use me, God, in Thy great harvest field,
Which stretcheth far and wide like a wide sea;
The gatherers are so few; I fear the precious yield
Will suffer loss. Oh, find a place for me!
A place where best the strength I have will tell:
It may be one the older toilers shun;
Be it a wide or narrow place, 'tis well
So that the work it holds be only done.

Christina Rossetti

THE GOSPEL OF LABOR

Yet often I think the king of that country,
　　comes out from His tireless host,
And walks in this world of the weary
　　as if He loved it the most;
For here in the dusty confusion,
　　with eyes that are heavy and dim,
He meets again the laboring men
　　who are looking and longing for Him.

He cancels the curse of Eden,
　　and brings them a blessing instead:
Blessed are they that labor,
　　for Jesus partakes of their bread,
He puts His hand to their burdens,
　　He enters their homes at night:
Who does his best shall have as his guest
　　the Master of life and light.

And courage will come with His presence,
　　and patience return at His touch,
And manifold sins be forgiven
　　to those who love Him much;
And the cries of envy and anger
　　will change to the songs of cheer,
For the toiling age will forget its rage
　　when the Prince of Peace draws near.

This is the gospel of labor,
　　ring it, ye bells of the kirk!
The Lord of Love comes down from above
　　to live with the men who work.
This is the rose that He planted,
　　here in the thorn-cursed soil:
Heaven is blessed with perfect rest,
　　but the blessing of earth is toil.

Henry van Dyke
237

SONNET VII

How soon hath Time the subtle thief of youth,
Stol'n on his wing my three and twentieth year!
My hasting days fly on with full career,
But my late spring no bud or blossom shew'th.
Perhaps my semblance might deceive the truth,
That I to manhood am arriv'd so near,
And inward ripeness doth much less appear,
That some more timely-happy spirits endu'th.
Yet be it less or more, or soon or slow,
It shall be still in strictest measure ev'n,
To that same lot, however mean, or high,
Toward which Time leads me, and the will of Heav'n;
All is, if I have grace to use it so,
As ever in my great Task-Master's eye.

John Milton

ODE TO DUTY

Stern Daughter of the Voice of God!
  O Duty! if that name thou love
Who are a light to guide, a rod
  To check the erring, and reprove;
Thou, who art victory and law
When empty terrors overawe,
From vain temptations dost set free,
And calm'st the weary strife of frail humanity!

There are who ask not if thine eye
  Be on them; who, in love and truth
Where no misgiving is, rely
  Upon the genial sense of youth:
Glad hearts! without reproach or blot,
Who do thy work, and know it not:
O! if through confidence misplaced
They fail, thy saving arms, dread Power! around them cast.

238

Serene will be our days and bright,
    And happy will our nature be,
When love is an unerring light,
    And joy its own security.
And they a blissful course may hold
Ev'n now, who, not unwisely bold,
Live in the spirit of this creed,
Yet seek thy firm support, according to their need.

I, loving freedom, and untried,
    No sport of every random gust,
Yet being to myself a guide,
    Too blindly have reposed my trust:
And oft, when in my heart was heard
Thy timely mandate, I deferr'd
The task, in smoother walks to stray;
But thee I now would serve more strictly, if I may.

Through no disturbance of my soul
    Or strong compunction in me wrought,
I supplicate for thy control,
    But in the quietness of thought:
Me this uncharter'd freedom tires;
I feel the weight of chance desires:
My hopes no more must change their name;
I long for a repose that ever is the same.

Stern Lawgiver! yet thou dost wear
    The Godhead's most benignant grace;
Nor know we anything so fair
    As in the smile upon thy face:
Flowers laugh before thee on their beds,
And fragrance in thy footing treads;
Thou dost preserve the stars from wrong;
And the most ancient heavens, through thee, are fresh and strong.

To humbler functions, awful Power!
   I call thee: I myself commend
Unto thy guidance from this hour;
   O let my weakness have an end!
Give unto me, made lowly wise,
   The spirit of self-sacrifice;
   The confidence of reason give;
And in the light of Truth thy bondman let me live.

William Wordsworth

FABLE

The mountain and the squirrel
Had a quarrel;
And the former called the latter "Little Prig."
Bun replied,
"You are doubtless very big;
But all sorts of things and weather
Must be taken in together
To make up a year
And a sphere.
And I think it's no disgrace
To occupy my place.
If I'm not so large as you,
You are not so small as I;
And not half so spry.
I'll not deny you make
A very pretty squirrel track;
Talents differ: all is well and wisely put;
If I cannot carry forests on my back,
Neither can you crack a nut."

Ralph Waldo Emerson

23. Friendship and Fellowship

THE BEST TREASURE

There are veins in the hills where jewels hide,
    And gold lies buried deep;
    There are harbor-towns where the great ships ride,
    And fame and fortune sleep;
But land and sea though we tireless rove,
And follow each trail to the end,
    Whatever the wealth of our treasure-trove,
The best we shall find is a friend.

John J. Moment

THE BLITHE MASK

He went so blithely on the way
    That people call the Road of Life,
That good folks, who had stopped to pray,
Shaking their heads would look and say
It wasn't right to be so gay
    Upon this weary road of strife.

He whistled as he went, and still
    He bore the young where streams were deep,
He helped the feeble up the hill;
He seemed to go with heart athrill,
Careless of deed and wild of will.
    He whistled that he might not weep.

Dollett Fuguet

ALL IN ALL

In Love, if Love be Love, if Love be ours,
Faith and unfaith can ne'er be equal powers:
Unfaith in aught is want of faith in all.

It is the little rift within the lute,
That by and by will make the music mute,
And ever widening slowly silence all.

The little rift within the lover's lute,
Or little pitted speck in garner'd fruit,
That rotting inward slowly moulders all.

It is not worth the keeping: let it go:
But shall it? answer, darling, answer, no.
And trust me not at all or all in all.

Alfred Tennyson

from *IN MEMORIAM*

Thy voice is on the rolling air;
    I hear thee where the waters run;
    Thou standest in the rising sun,
And in the setting thou art fair.

What art thou then? I cannot guess;
    But tho' I seem in star and flower
    To feel thee some diffusive power,
I do not therefore love thee less:

My love involves the love before;
    My love is vaster passion now;
    Tho' mix'd with God and Nature thou,
I seem to love thee more and more.

242

Far off thou art, but ever nigh;
   I have thee still, and I rejoice;
   I prosper, circled with thy voice;
I shall not lose thee tho' I die.

Alfred Tennyson

REMEMBRANCE

When to the session of sweet silent thought,
I summon up remembrance of things past,
I sign the lack of many a thing I sought,
And with old woes new wail my dear time's waste;
Then can I drown an eye, unused to flow,
For precious friends hid in death's dateless night,
And weep afresh love's long-since-cancelled woe,
And moan the expense of many a vanished sight.
Then can I grieve at grievances foregone,
And heavily from woe to woe tell o'er
The sad account of fore-bemoaned moan,
Which I now pay as if not paid before:
But if the while I think on thee, dear friend,
All losses are restored, and sorrows end.

William Shakespeare

THE HOUSE BY THE SIDE OF THE ROAD

There are hermit souls that live withdrawn
   In the place of their self-content;
There are souls like stars, that dwell apart,
   In a fellowless firmament;
There are pioneer souls that blaze their paths
   Where highways never ran—
But let me live by the side of the road
   And be a friend to man.

243

Let me live in a house by the side of the road,
    Where the race of men go by—
The men who are good and the men who are bad,
    As good and as bad as I.
I would not sit in the scorner's seat,
    Or hurl the cynic's ban—
Let me live in a house by the side of the road
    And be a friend to man.

I see from my house by the side of the road,
    By the side of the highway of life,
The men who press with the ardor of hope,
    The men who are faint with the strife.
But I turn not away from their smiles nor their tears,
    Both parts of an infinite plan—
Let me live in a house by the side of the road
    And be a friend to man.

I know there are brook-gladdened meadows ahead
    And mountains of wearisome height;
That the road passes on through the long afternoon
    And stretches away to the night.
But still I rejoice when the travelers rejoice,
    And weep with the strangers that moan,
Nor live in my house by the side of the road
    Like a man who dwells alone.

Let me live in my house by the side of the road—
    It's here the race of men go by.
They are good, they are bad, they are weak, they are strong
    Wise, foolish—so am I;
Then why should I sit in the scorner's seat,
    Or hurl the cynic's ban?
Let me live in my house by the side of the road
    And be a friend to man.

Sam Walter Foss

I SOUGHT MY SOUL

I sought my soul,
　　But my soul I could not see.
I sought my God,
　　But my God eluded me.
I sought my brother,
　　And I found all three.

Author unknown

FROM *ULYSSES*

Come, my friends
'Tis not too late to seek a newer world.
Push off, and sitting well in order smite
The sounding furrows; for my purpose holds
To sail beyond the sunset, and the baths
Of all the western stars, until I die.
It may be that the gulfs will wash us down;
It may be we shall touch the Happy Isles,
And see the great Achilles, whom we knew.
Tho' much is taken, much abides; and tho'
We are not now that strength which in old days
Moved earth and heaven; that which we are, we are;
One equal temper of heroic hearts,
Made weak by time and fate, but strong in will
To strive, to seek, to find, and not to yield.

Alfred Tennyson

MAKE FRIENDS

He who has a thousand friends has not a friend to spare,
And he who has one enemy shall meet him everywhere.

Ali Ben Abu Taleb

245

THE ONE HUNDRED AND THIRTY-THIRD PSALM

Behold how good and how pleasant it is
  for brethren to dwell together in unity!
It is like the precious ointment upon the head,
    that ran down upon the beard, even Aaron's beard:
      that went down to the skirts of his garments.
As the dew of Hermon,
    and as the dew that descended
      upon the mountains of Zion,
        for there the Lord commanded the blessing:
          even life for evermore.

IF I CAN STOP ONE HEART FROM BREAKING

If I can stop one heart from breaking,
I shall not live in vain;
If I can ease one life the aching,
Or cool one pain,
Or help one fainting robin
Unto his nest again,
I shall not live in vain.

Emily Dickinson

THERE IS A LOVE

There is a love that tumbles like a stream,
Frothing and foaming down a budded way;
There is a love like ocean depths that move
Hidden, eternal—winter as in May.

There is a love that stumbles through its lines
Trying to say what love can never say;
There is another—patient, tender, strong—
Serving and blessing till the close of day.

Philip Jerome Cleveland

24.   Praise and Thanksgiving

I SING THE MIGHTY POWER OF GOD

I sing the mighty power of God,
That made the mountains rise,
That spread the flowing seas abroad,
And built the lofty skies.
I sing the wisdom that ordained
The sun to rule the day;
The moon shines full at his command,
And all the stars obey.

I sing the goodness of the Lord,
That filled the earth with food;
He formed the creatures with his word,
And then pronounced them good.
Lord, how thy wonders are displayed,
Where'er I turn my eye:
If I survey the ground I tread,
Or gaze upon the sky!

There's not a plant or flower below,
But makes thy glories known;
And clouds arise, and tempests blow,
By order from thy throne,
While all that borrows life from thee
Is ever in thy care,
And everywhere that man can be,
Thou, God, art present there.

Isaac Watts

THANKSGIVING

For all true words that have been spoken,
    For all brave deeds that have been done,
For every loaf in kindness broken,
    For every race in valor run,
For martyr lips which have not failed
    To give God praise and smile to rest,
For knightly souls which have not quailed
    At stubborn strife or lonesome quest;
Lord unto whom we stand in thrall
    We give Thee thanks for all, for all.

For each fair field where golden stubble
    Hath followed wealth of waving grain;
For every passing wind of trouble
    Which bends Thy grass that lifts again;
For gold in mine that men must seek,
    For work which bows the sullen knee;
For strength, swift sent to aid the weak,
    For love by which we climb to Thee;
Thy freemen, Lord, yet each Thy thrall,
    We give Thee praise for all, for all.

Margaret E. Sangster

A SUN-DAY HYMN

Lord of all being! throned afar,
Thy glory flames from sun and star;
Centre and soul of every sphere,
Yet to each loving heart how near!

Sun of our life, thy quickening ray
Sheds on our path the glow of day;
Star of our hope, thy softened light
Cheers the long watches of the night.

Our midnight is thy smile withdrawn;
Our noontide is thy gracious dawn;
Our rainbow arch thy mercy's sign;
All, save the clouds of sin, are thine!

Lord of all life, below, above,
Whose light is truth, whose warmth is love,
Before thy ever-blazing throne
We ask no lustre of our own.

Grant us thy truth to make us free,
And kindling hearts that burn for thee,
Till all thy living altars claim
One holy light, one heavenly flame!

Oliver Wendell Holmes

THE SUMMER DAYS ARE COME AGAIN

The summer days are come again;
    Once more the glad earth yields
Her golden wealth of ripening grain,
    And breath of clover fields,
And deepening shade of summer woods,
    And glow of summer air,
And winging thoughts, and happy moods
    Of love and joy and prayer.

The summer days are come again;
    The birds are on the wing;
God's praises, in their loving strain,
    Unconsciously they sing.
We know who giveth all the good
    That doth our cup o'erbrim;
For summer joy in field and wood
    We lift our song to Him.

Samuel Longfellow
249

TO A BIRD AFTER A STORM

Hither thou com'st: the busy wind all night
Blew through thy lodging, where thine own warm wing
Thy pillow was. Many a sullen storm,
For which coarse man seems much the fitter born,
    Rain'd on thy bed
    And harmless head.

And now as fresh and cheerful as the light
Thy little heart in early hymns doth sing
Unto that Providence, Whose unseen arm
Curb'd them, and cloth'd thee well and warm.
    All things that be praise Him; and had
    Their lesson taught them when first made.

So hills and valleys into singing break;
And though poor stones have neither speech nor tongue,
While active winds and streams both run and speak,
Yet stones are deep in admiration.
    Thus praise and prayer here beneath the sun
    Make lesser mornings, when the great are done.

Henry Vaughan

THE BURNING BUSH

I will now turn aside and see this great sight.—EXODUS 3:3

    Thy wisdom and Thy might appear,
    Eternal God, through every year;
    From day to day, from hour to hour,
    Thy works reveal self-ordered power.

    We worship Thee whose will hath laid
    Thy sovereign rule on all things made;
    The faithful stars, the fruitful earth,
    Obey Thy laws that gave them birth.

Yet Thou canst make a marvel shine
Amid these mighty laws of Thine,
As when Thy servant Moses came
And saw the bush with Thee aflame.

We turn aside and tread the ways
That lead through wonder up to praise;
Wherever Thou by man art found
The homely earth is holy ground.

If Thou hast formed us out of dust
Through ages long,—in Thee we trust;
O grant us in our souls to see
The living flame that comes from Thee.

Henry van Dyke

FROM *A LITTLE TE DEUM OF THE COMMONPLACE*

For all Thy ministries,—
For morning mist, and gently-falling dew;
For summer rains, for winter ice and snow;
For whispering wind and purifying storm;
For the reft clouds that show the tender blue;
For the forked flash and long tumultuous roll;
For mighty rains that wash the dim earth clean;
For the sweet promise of the seven-fold bow;
For the soft sunshine, and the still calm night;
For dimpled laughter of soft summer seas;
For latticed splendour of the sea-borne moon;
For gleaming sands, and granite-frontled cliffs;
For flying spume, and waves that whip the skies;
For rushing gale, and for the great glad calm;
For Might so mighty, and for Love so true,
With equal mind,
    We thank Thee, Lord!

John Oxenham

FROM *A SONG TO DAVID*

He sang of God—the mighty source
Of all things—the stupendous force
   On which all strength depends;
From Whose right arm, beneath Whose eyes,
All period, power, and enterprise
   Commences, reigns, and ends.

     *   *   *

O David, scholar of the Lord!
Such is thy science, whence reward,
   And infinite degree;
O strength, O sweetness, lasting ripe!
God's harp thy symbol, and thy type
   The lion and the bee!

There is but One who ne'er rebelled,
But One by passion unimpelled,
   By pleasures unenticed;
He from himself hath semblance sent,
Grand object of his own content,
   And saw the God in Christ.

Tell them, I AM, Jehovah said
To Moses; while earth heard in dread,
   And, smitten to the heart,
At once above, beneath, around,
All Nature, without voice or sound,
   Replied, 'O Lord, THOU ART.'

                     Christopher Smart

FROM *IN MEMORY OF W. B. YEATS*

Follow, poet, follow right
To the bottom of the night,
With your unconstraining voice
Still persuade us to rejoice;

With the farming of a verse
Make a vineyard of the curse,
Sing of human unsuccess
In a rapture of distress;

In the deserts of the heart
Let the healing fountain start,
In the prison of his days
Teach the free man how to praise.

W. H. Auden

THE ONE HUNDREDTH PSALM

Make a joyful noise unto the Lord, all ye lands.
Serve the Lord with gladness:
   come before his presence with singing.
Know ye that the Lord, he is God:
   it is he that hath made us,
      and not we ourselves:
         we are his people,
            and the sheep of his pasture.
Enter into his gates with thanksgiving,
   and into his courts with praise:
      be thankful unto him,
         and bless his name.
For the Lord is good;
   his mercy is everlasting:
      and his truth endureth to all generations.

FROM OUR PRAYER OF THANKS

For the gladness here where the sun is shining at evening
      on the weeds at the river,
                Our prayer of thanks.
For the laughter of children who tumble barefooted and bareheaded
    in the summer grass,
                Our prayer of thanks.

Carl Sandburg

FATHER, HOW WIDE THY GLORIES SHINE

Father, how wide thy glories shine,
God of the universe, and mine!
Thy goodness watches o'er the whole,
As all mankind were but one soul,
Yet keeps my every sacred hair,
As I remain'd thy single care.

Charles Wesley

THE ONE HUNDRED AND FIFTIETH PSALM

Praise ye the Lord.
Praise God in his sanctuary:
  praise him in the firmament of his power.
Praise him for his mighty acts:
  praise him according to his excellent greatness.
Praise him with the sound of the trumpet:
  praise him with the psaltery and harp.
Praise him with the timbrel and dance:
  praise him with stringed instruments and organs.
Praise him upon the loud cymbals:
  praise him upon the high sounding cymbals.
Let every thing that hath breath praise the Lord.
Praise ye the Lord.

254

TO HIM BE GLORY

O depth of wealth, wisdom, and knowledge in God!
How unsearchable his judgements, how untraceable his ways!
Who knows the mind of the Lord?
Who has been his counsellor?
Who has ever made a gift to him, to receive a gift in return?
Source, Guide, and Goal of all that is—
    to him be glory for ever! Amen.

Paul (Romans 12:33-36, *The New English Bible*)

HAVE WE NOT SEEN THY SHINING GARMENT'S HEM

Have we not seen Thy shining garment's hem
Floating at dawn across the golden skies,
Through thin blue veils at noon, bright majesties,
Seen starry hosts delight to gem
The splendour that shall be Thy diadem?

    O Immanence, that knows nor far nor near,
    But as the air we breathe is with us here,
    Our Breath of Life, O Lord, we worship Thee.

Worship and laud and praise Thee evermore,
Look up in wonder, and behold a door
Opened in heaven, and One set on a throne;
Stretch out a hand, and touch Thine own,
O Christ, our King, our Lord whom we adore.

Amy Carmichael

255

PRAISE

What do they know of penitence
    Who never wrought Him wrong?
How can the sinless lift to Him
    Redemption's triumph-song?

There lies an eloquence of praise
    Imprisoned in a tear
And crushed within a broken heart
    That God bends low to hear.

Edith Daley

FROM ALL THAT DWELL BELOW THE SKIES

From all that dwell below the skies
    Let the Creator's praise arise!
Let the Redeemer's name be sung
    Through every land, by every tongue!

Eternal are Thy mercies, Lord,
    Eternal truth attends Thy Word:
Thy praise shall sound from shore to shore
    Till suns shall rise and set no more.

Isaac Watts

A HEART TO PRAISE THEE

Thou hast given so much to me,
Give one thing more—a grateful heart:
Not thankful when it pleaseth me,
As if thy blessings had spare days,
But such a heart whose Pulse may be
Thy Praise.

George Herbert

V

THE REIGN
OF GOD

25. *Bless This House*

BLESS THIS HOUSE

Bless this house, O Lord, we pray,
   Make it safe by night and day;
Bless these walls, so firm and stout,
   Keeping want and trouble out;
Bless the roof and chimneys tall,
   Let thy peace lie over all;
Bless this door, that it may prove
   Ever open to joy and love.

Helen Taylor

THE ONE HUNDRED AND TWENTY-SEVENTH PSALM

Except the Lord build the house,
   they labour in vain that build it:
     except the Lord keep the city,
      the watchman waketh but in vain.
It is vain for you to rise up early,
   to sit up late,
     to eat the bread of sorrows:
      for so he giveth his beloved sleep.
Lo, children are an heritage of the Lord:
   and the fruit of the womb is his reward.
As arrows are in the hand of a mighty man:
   so are the children of youth.
Happy is the man that hath his quiver full of them;
   they shall not be ashamed:
     but they shall speak with the enemies in the gate.

HOME
FROM *THE DEATH OF THE HIRED MAN*

"Home is the place where, when you have to go there,
They have to take you in."
                    "I should have called it
Something you somehow haven't to deserve."

Robert Frost

HOUSE AND HOME

A house is built of logs and stone,
    Of tiles and posts and piers;
A home is built of loving deeds
    That stand a thousand years.

Victor Hugo

FROM *PRAYER FOR THE HOME*

Lord, this humble house we'd keep
Sweet with play and calm with sleep.
Help us so that we may give
Beauty to the lives we live.
Let Thy love and let Thy grace
Shine upon our dwelling place.

Edgar A. Guest

PEACE

"My peace," the peace of the Lord Most High,
    The peace of the Master passing by.
Be this in our home, by night, by day,
    Be this our joy if we go or stay.

Margaret E. Sangster

SEARCH

I sought Him in a great cathedral, dim
With age, where oft-repeated prayers arise,
But caught no glimpse of Him.

I sought Him then atop a lonely hill,
Like Moses once, but though I scanned the skies,
My search was fruitless still.

There was a little home where grief and care
Had bred but courage, love, and valiant will,
I sought—and found Him there.

Anne Marriott

FROM *A LITTLE TE DEUM OF THE COMMONPLACE*

For maiden sweetness, and for strength of men;
For love's pure madness and its high estate;
For parentage—man's nearest reach to Thee;
For kinship, sonship, friendship, brotherhood
Of men—one Father—one great family;
For glimpses of the greater in the less;
For touch of Thee in wife and child and friend;
For noble self-denying motherhood;
For saintly maiden lives of rare perfume;
For little pattering feet and crooning songs;
For children's laughter, and sweet wells of truth;
For sweet child-faces and the sweet wise tongues;
For childhood's faith that lifts us near to Thee
And bows us with our own disparity;
For childhood's sweet unconscious beauty sleep;
For all that childhood teaches us of Thee:
    We thank Thee, Lord!

John Oxenham

261

A PRAYER FOR THE HOUSEHOLD

Lord, behold our family here assembled.
We thank Thee for this place in which we dwell;
    for the love that unites us;
    for the peace accorded us this day;
    for the hope with which we expect the morrow;
    for the health, the work, the food and the bright skies
        that make our lives delightful;
    for our friends in all parts of the earth,
        and our friendly helpers in this foreign isle.
Let peace abound in our small company.
    Purge out of every heart the lurking grudge.
    Give us grace and strength to forbear and to persevere.
    Offenders,
        give us the grace to accept and to forgive offenders.
    Forgetful ourselves,
        help us to bear cheerfully the forgetfulness of others.
Give us courage and gaiety and the quiet mind.
    Spare to us our friends, soften to us our enemies.
    Bless us, if it may be, in all our innocent endeavors.
    If it may not,
        give us the strength to encounter that which is to come,
        that we be brave in peril,
        constant in tribulation,
        temperate in wrath and in all changes of fortune,
        and down to the gates of death loyal and loving one to
            another.
As the clay to the potter,
    as the windmill to the wind,
    as children of their sire,
    we beseech of Thee this help and mercy for Christ's sake.

Robert Louis Stevenson

THE HOUSEWIFE

Jesus, teach me how to be
Proud of my simplicity.

Sweep the floors, wash the clothes,
Gather for each vase a rose.

Iron and mend a tiny frock,
Keeping one eye on the clock.

Always having time kept free
For childish questions asked of me.

Grant me wisdom Mary had
When she taught her little Lad.

Catherine Cate Coblentz

A VIRTUOUS WOMAN

Who can find a virtuous woman?
    for her price is far above rubies.
The heart of her husband doth safely trust in her,
    so that he shall have no need of spoil.
        She will do him good and not evil all the days of her life.

       *   *   *

She looketh well to the ways of her household,
    and eateth not the bread of idleness.
Her children arise up, and call her blessed;
    her husband also, and he praiseth her.
Many daughters have done virtuously,
    but thou excellest them all.
Favour is deceitful, and beauty is vain:
    but a woman that feareth the Lord, she shall be praised.
Give her of the fruit of her hands;
    and let her own works praise her in the gates.

Proverbs 31:10-12, 27-31

263

THE OPEN DOOR

You, my son,
Have shown me God.
Your kiss upon my cheek
Has made me feel the gentle touch
Of Him who leads us on.
The memory of your smile, when young,
Reveals His face,
As mellowing years come on apace.
And when you went before,
You left the gates of heaven ajar
That I might glimpse,
Approaching from afar,
The glories of His grace.
Hold, son, my hand,
Guide me along the path,
That, coming,
I may stumble not,
Nor roam,
Nor fail to show the way
Which leads us home.

Grace Coolidge

THEY MIGHT NOT NEED ME; BUT THEY MIGHT

They might not need me; but they might.
I'll let my head be just in sight;
A smile as small as mine might be
Precisely their necessity.

Emily Dickinson

THE LITTLE POEM OF LIFE

I;—
Thou;—

                    We;—
                        They;—
Small words, but mighty.
In their span
Are bound the life and hopes of man.

For, first, his thoughts of his own self are full;
Until another comes his heart to rule.
For them, life's best is centred round their love;
Till younger lives come all their love to prove.

John Oxenham

THE HUNDRED AND TWENTY-EIGHTH PSALM

Blessed is every one that feareth the Lord:
   that walketh in his ways.
For thou shalt eat the labour of thine hands:
   happy shalt thou be, and it shall be well with thee.
Thy wife shall be as a fruitful vine
   by the sides of thine house,
     thy children like olive plants
       round about thy table.
Behold that thus shall the man be blessed
   that feareth the Lord.
The Lord shall bless thee out of Zion:
   and thou shalt see the good of Jerusalem,
     all the days of thy life.
Yea, thou shalt see thy children's children:
   and peace upon Israel.

IN THINE ARMS

Our families in Thine arms enfold
As Thou didst keep Thy folk of old.

Oliver Wendell Holmes

26. Love in the Home

HOW DO I LOVE THEE?

How do I love thee? Let me count the ways.
I love thee to the depth and breadth and height
My soul can reach, when feeling out of sight
For the ends of Being and ideal Grace.
I love thee to the level of everyday's
Most quiet need, by sun and candle-light.
I love thee freely, as men strive for Right;
I love thee purely, as they turn from Praise.
I love thee with the passion put to use
In my old griefs, and with my childhood's faith.
I love thee with a love I seemed to lose
With my lost saints,—I love thee with the breath,
Smiles, tears, of all my life!—and, if God choose,
I shall but love thee better after death.

Elizabeth Barrett Browning

FROM THE SONG OF HIAWATHA

As the bow unto the cord is
So unto the man is woman.
Though she bends him, she obeys him,
Though she draws him, yet she follows,
Useless each without the other.

Henry Wadsworth Longfellow

SONNET TWENTY-NINE

When in disgrace with fortune and men's eyes
I all alone beweep my outcast state,
And trouble deaf heaven with my bootless cries,
And look upon myself and curse my fate,
Wishing me like to one more rich in hope,
Featured like him, like him with friends possessed,
Desiring this man's art, and that man's scope,
Wish what I most enjoy contented least;
Yet in these thoughts myself almost despising,
Haply I think on thee—and then my state,
Like to the lark at break of day arising
From sullen earth, sings hymns at heaven's gate:
    For thy sweet love remembered, such wealth brings
    That then I scorn to change my state with kings.

William Shakespeare

TO MY WIFE

Trusty, dusky, vivid, true,
With eyes of gold and bramble-dew,
Steel true and blade straight
The Great Artificer made my mate.

Honor, anger, valor, fire,
A love that life could never tire,
Death quench nor evil stir,
The Mighty Master gave to her.

Teacher, tender comrade, wife,
A fellow-farer true through life,
Heart-whole and soul-free,
The August Father gave to me.

Robert Louis Stevenson

ENTREAT ME NOT TO LEAVE THEE

Entreat me not to leave thee,
 or to return from following after thee:
For whither thou goest, I will go;
 and where thou lodgest, I will lodge:
Thy people shall be my people,
 and thy God my God:
Where thou diest, will I die,
 and there will I be buried:
The Lord do so to me, and more also,
 if aught but death part thee and me.

Ruth, to Naomi (Ruth 1:16-17)

MOTHER O' MINE

If I were hanged on the highest hill,
 Mother o' mine, O mother o' mine!
I know whose love would follow me still,
 Mother o' mine, O mother o' mine!
If I were drowned in the deepest sea,
 Mother o' mine, O mother o' mine!
I know whose tears would come down to me,
 Mother o' mine, O mother o' mine!
If I were damned o' body and soul,
I know whose prayers would make me whole,
 Mother o' mine, O mother o' mine!

Rudyard Kipling

I FOUND GOD

Sophisticated, worldly-wise,
I searched for God and found Him not,
Until one day, the world forgot,
I found Him in my baby's eyes.

Mary Afton Thacker

A CHILD'S THOUGHT OF GOD

They say that God lives very high!
But if you look above the pines
You cannot see our God. And why?

And if you dig down in the mines
You never see Him in the gold,
Though from Him all that's glory shines.

God is so good, He wears a fold
Of heaven and earth across His face—
Like secrets kept, for love, untold.

But still I feel that His embrace
Slides down by thrills, through all things made,
Through sight and sound of every place:

As if my tender mother laid
On my shut lids, her kisses' pressure,
Half waking me at night; and said,
"Who kissed you through the dark, dear guesser?"

Elizabeth Barrett Browning

BABY

Where did you come from, baby dear?
Out of the everywhere into here.

Where did you get those eyes so blue?
Out of the sky as I came through.

What makes the light in them sparkle and spin?
Some of the starry spikes left in.

Where did you get that little tear?
I found it waiting when I got here.

269

What makes your forehead so smooth and high?
A soft hand stroked it as I went by.

What makes your cheek like a warm white rose?
I saw something better than any one knows.

Whence that three-cornered smile of bliss?
Three angels gave me at once a kiss.

Where did you get this pearly ear?
God spoke, and it came out to hear.

Where did you get those arms and hands?
Love made itself into bonds and bands.

Feet, whence did you come, you darling things?
From the same box as the cherubs' wings.

How did they all just come to be you?
God thought about me, and so I grew.

But how did you come to us, you dear?
God thought about you, and so I am here.

George Macdonald

FROM *ODE ON INTIMATIONS OF IMMORTALITY*

Our birth is but a sleep and a forgetting;
The Soul that rises with us, our Life's Star,
Hath had elsewhere its setting
And cometh from afar;
Not in entire forgetfulness,
And not in utter nakedness,
But trailing clouds of glory do we come
From God, who is our home:
Heaven lies about us in our infancy!

William Wordsworth

270

LOVE

I love you
Not only for what you are,
But for what I am
When I am with you.

I love you,
Not only for what
You have made of yourself,
But for what
You are making of me.

I love you
For the part of me
That you bring out;
I love you
For putting your hand
Into my heaped-up heart
And passing over
All the foolish, weak things
That you can't help
Dimly seeing there,
And for drawing out
Into the light
All the beautiful belongings
That no one else had looked
Quite far enough to find.

I love you because you
Are helping me to make
Of the lumber of my life
Not a tavern
But a temple;
Out of the works
Of my every day
Not a reproach
But a song. . . .

Mary Carolyn Davies

27. Nation Under God

PLEDGE OF ALLEGIANCE

I pledge allegiance
to the flag of the United States of America
and to the republic for which it stands:
one nation under God,
indivisible,
with liberty and justice for all.

THE NEW COLOSSUS

Not like the brazen giant of Greek fame,
With conquering limbs astride from land to land;
Here at our sea-washed, sunset gates shall stand
A mighty woman with a torch, whose flame
Is the imprisoned lightning, and her name
Mother of Exiles. From her beacon-hand
Glows world-wide welcome; her mild eyes command
The air-bridged harbor that twin cities frame.
"Keep, ancient lands, your storied pomp!" cries she
With silent lips. "Give me your tired, your poor,
Your huddled masses yearning to breathe free,
The wretched refuse of your teeming shore,
Send these, the homeless, tempest-tost to me,
I lift my lamp beside the golden door."

Emma Lazarus

RECESSIONAL

God of our fathers, known of old—
  Lord of our far-flung battle-line—
Beneath whose awful Hand we hold
  Dominion over palm and pine—
Lord God of Hosts, be with us yet,
Lest we forget, lest we forget!

The tumult and the shouting dies—
  The captains and the kings depart—
Still stands Thine ancient sacrifice,
  An humble and a contrite heart.
Lord God of Hosts, be with us yet,
Lest we forget, lest we forget!

Far-call'd our navies melt away—
  On dune and headland sinks the fire—
Lo, all our pomp of yesterday
  Is one with Nineveh and Tyre!
Judge of the Nations, spare us yet,
Lest we forget, lest we forget!

If, drunk with sight of power, we loose
  Wild tongues that have not Thee in awe—
Such boasting as the Gentiles use
  Or lesser breeds without the Law—
Lord God of Hosts, be with us yet,
Lest we forget, lest we forget!

For heathen heart that puts her trust
  In reeking tube and iron shard—
All valiant dust that builds on dust,
  And guarding calls not Thee to guard—
For frantic boast and foolish word,
Thy Mercy on Thy People, Lord!

Rudyard Kipling

UNMANIFEST DESTINY

To what new fates, my country, far
    And unforeseen of foe or friend,
Beneath what unexpected star
    Compelled to what unchosen end,

Across the sea that knows no beach,
    The Admiral of Nations guides
Thy blind obedient keels to reach
    The harbor where thy future rides!

The guns that spoke at Lexington
    Knew not that God was planning then
The trumpet word of Jefferson
    To bugle forth the rights of men.

To them that wept and cursed Bull Run,
    What was it but despair and shame?
Who saw behind the cloud the sun?
    Who knew that God was in the flame?

Had not defeat upon defeat,
    Disaster on disaster come,
The slave's emancipated feet
    Had never marched behind the drum.

There is a Hand that bends our deeds
    To mightier issues than we planned;
Each son that triumphs, each that bleeds,
    My country, serves Its dark command.

I do not know beneath what sky
    Nor on what seas shall be thy fate;
I only know it shall be high,
    I only know it shall be great.

Richard Hovey

PEACE HYMN OF THE REPUBLIC

O Lord, our God, Thy mighty hand
    Hath made our country free;
From all her broad and happy land
    May praise arise to Thee.
Fulfil the promise of her youth,
    Her liberty defend;
By law and order, love and truth,
    America befriend!

The strength of every state increase
    In Union's golden chain;
Her thousand cities fill with peace,
    Her million fields with grain.
The virtues of her mingled blood
    In one new people blend;
By unity and brotherhood
    America befriend!

O suffer not her feet to stray;
    But guide her untaught might,
That she may walk in peaceful day,
    And lead the world in light.
Bring down the proud, lift up the poor,
    Unequal ways amend;
By justice, nation-wide and sure,
    America befriend!

Through all the waiting land proclaim
    Thy gospel of good-will;
And may the music of Thy name
    In every bosom thrill.
O'er hill and vale, from sea to sea,
    Thy holy reign extend;
By faith and hope and charity,
    America befriend!

Henry van Dyke

FROM *LETTER TO THE GOVERNORS, JUNE 8, 1783*

I now make it my earnest prayer
that God would have you,
and the state over which you preside, in His holy protection;
that He would incline the hearts of the citizens
to cultivate a spirit of subordination and obedience
    to the government;
to entertain a brotherly affection and love for one another,
for their fellow citizens of the United States at large
and particularly for their brethren who have served in the field;
and finally
that He would graciously be pleased to dispose us all
    to do justice,
to love mercy,
and to demean ourselves with charity and humility,
and a pacific temper of mind,
which were characteristics of the Divine Author
    of our blessed religion,
and without an humble imitation of whose example in these things,
we can never hope to be a happy nation.

George Washington

FROM *GOD SEND US MEN*

God send us men with hearts ablaze,
    All truth to love, all wrong to hate;
These are the patriots nations need,
    These are the bulwarks of the State.

F. J. Gillman

THE GETTYSBURG ADDRESS

Fourscore and seven years ago
our fathers brought forth on this continent a new nation,

276

conceived in liberty,
and dedicated to the proposition
that all men are created equal.

   Now we are engaged in a great civil war,
testing whether that nation,
or any nation so conceived and so dedicated,
can long endure.
We are met on a great battlefield of that war.
We have come to dedicate a portion of that field
as a final resting place
of those who here gave their lives
that this nation might live.
It is altogether fitting and proper that we should do this.

   But in a larger sense,
we cannot dedicate—
we cannot consecrate—
we cannot hallow this ground.
The brave men, living and dead, who struggled here,
have consecrated it far above our poor power to add or detract.
The world will little note nor long remember
what we say here,
but it can never forget what they did here.
It is for us, the living,
rather, to be dedicated here to the unfinished work
they who fought here have thus far so nobly advanced.
It is rather for us to be here dedicated
to the great task remaining before us—
that from these honored dead we take increased devotion
to that cause for which they gave the last full measure of devotion;
that we here highly resolve that these dead shall not have died in
    vain;
that this nation, under God, shall have a new birth of freedom;
and that government of the people,
by the people,
for the people,
shall not perish from the earth.

Abraham Lincoln
277

FOUR THINGS

Four things in any land must dwell,
If it endures and prospers well:
One is manhood true and good;
One is noble womanhood;
One is child life, clean and bright;
And one an altar kept alight.

Author unknown

PATRIOTISM

Breathes there a man with soul so dead
Who never to himself hath said,
"This is my own, my native land!"
Whose heart hath ne'er within him burned
As home his footsteps he hath turned
From wandering on a foreign strand?
If such there breathe, go, mark him well!
For him no minstrel raptures swell;
High though his titles, power, and pelf,
The wretch, concentred all in self,
Living, shall forfeit fair renown,
And, doubly dying, shall go down
To the vile dust from whence he sprung,
Unwept, unhonored, and unsung.

Sir Walter Scott

LET US HAVE FAITH THAT RIGHT MAKES MIGHT

Let us have faith that right makes might;
and in that faith
let us to the end dare to do our duty
as we understand it.

Abraham Lincoln

FROM *THE DESERTED VILLAGE*

Ill fares the land, to hastening ills a prey,
Where wealth accumulates, and men decay.

Oliver Goldsmith

A NATION'S STRENGTH

What makes a nation's pillars high
   And its foundations strong?
What makes it mighty to defy
   The foes that round it throng?

It is not gold. Its kingdoms grand
   Go down in battle shock;
Its shafts are laid on sinking sand,
   Not on abiding rock.

Is it the sword? Ask the red dust
   Of empires passed away;
The blood has turned their stones to rust,
   Their glory to decay.

And is it pride? Ah, that bright crown
   Has seemed to nations sweet;
But God has struck its luster down
   In ashes at His feet.

Not gold but only men can make
   A people great and strong;
Men who for truth and honor's sake
   Stand fast and suffer long.

Brave men who work while others sleep,
   Who dare while others fly—

279

They build a nation's pillars deep
   And lift them to the sky.

Ralph Waldo Emerson

BOSTON HYMN

The word of the Lord by night
To the watching Pilgrims came,
As they sat by the seaside,
And filled their hearts with flame.

God said, I am tired of kings,
I suffer them no more;
Up to my ear the morning brings
The outrage of the poor.

Think ye I made this ball
A field of havoc and war,
Where tyrants great and tyrants small
Might harry the weak and poor?

My angel,—his name is Freedom,—
Choose him to be your king;
He shall cut pathways east and west
And fend you with his wing.

Lo! I uncover the land
Which I hid of old time in the West,
As the sculptor uncovers the statue
When he has wrought his best;

I show Columbia, of the rocks
Which dip their foot in the seas
And soar to the air-borne flocks
Of clouds and the boreal fleece.

I will divide my goods;
Call in the wretch and slave:
None shall rule but the humble,
And none but Toil shall have.

I will have never a noble,
No lineage counted great;
Fishers and choppers and ploughmen
Shall constitute a state.

Go, cut down trees in the forest
And trim the straightest boughs;
Cut down trees in the forest
And build me a wooden house.

Call the people together,
The young men and the sires,
The digger in the harvest-field,
Hireling and him that hires;

And here in a pine state-house
They shall choose men to rule
In every needful faculty,
In church and state and school.

Lo now! if these poor men
Can govern the land and sea
And make just laws below the sun,
As planets faithful be.

And ye shall succor men;
'Tis nobleness to serve;
Help them who cannot help again:
Beware from right to swerve.

I break your bonds and masterships,
And I unchain the slave:

Free be his heart and hand henceforth
As wind and wandering wave.

I cause from every creature
His proper good to flow:
As much as he is and doeth,
So much he shall bestow.

But, lay hands on another
To coin his labor and sweat,
He goes in pawn for his victim
For eternal years in debt.

Today unbind the captive,
So only are ye unbound;
Lift up a people from the dust,
Trump of their rescue, sound!

Pay ransom to the owner
And fill the bag to the brim.
Who is the owner? The slave is owner,
And ever was. Pay him.

O North! give him beauty for rags,
And honor, O South! for his shame;
Nevada! coin thy golden crags
With Freedom's image and name.

Up! and the dusky race
That sat in darkness long,—
Be swift their feet as antelopes,
And as behemoth strong.

Come, East and West and North,
By races, as snow flakes,
And carry my purpose forth,
Which neither halts nor shakes.

My will fulfilled shall be,
For, in daylight or in dark,
My thunderbolt has eyes to see
His way home to the mark.

Ralph Waldo Emerson

MINE EYES HAVE SEEN THE GLORY

Mine eyes have seen the glory of the coming of the Lord:
He is trampling out the vintage
    where the grapes of wrath are stored;
He hath loosed the fateful lightning
    of his terrible swift sword:
  His truth is marching on.

I have seen him in the watch-fires of a hundred circling camps,
They have builded him an altar in the evening dews and damps;
I can read his righteous sentence by the dim and flaring lamps:
  His day is marching on.

I have read a fiery gospel writ in burnished rows of steel:
"As ye deal with my contemners so with you my grace shall deal;
Let the Hero, born of woman, crush the serpent with his heel,
  Since God is marching on!"

He has sounded forth the trumpet that shall never call retreat;
He is sifting out the hearts of men before His judgment seat.
Oh, be swift, my soul, to answer Him! be jubilant, my feet!
  Our God is marching on.

In the beauty of the lilies Christ was born across the sea,
With a glory in His bosom that transfigures you and me;
As He died to make men holy, let us die to make men free,
  While God is marching on.

Julia Ward Howe

28. The Church

AN ANGEL UNAWARES

If after kirk ye bide a wee,
There's some would like to speak to ye;
If after kirk ye rise and flee,
We'll all seem cold and stiff to ye.
The one that's in the seat wi' ye,
Is stranger here than you, may be;
All here hae got their fears and cares—
Add you your soul unto our prayers;
Be you our angel unawares.

Author unknown

GOD'S SAINTS

God's saints are shining lights; who stays
    Here long must pass
O'er dark hills, swift streams and steep ways
    As smooth as glass:
    But these all night,
    Like candles, shed
    Their beams and light
    Us into bed.
They are—indeed—our pillar fires
    Seen as we go;
They are that City's shining spires
    We travel to.

Henry Vaughan

WE LOVE THE VENERABLE HOUSE

We love the venerable house
Our fathers built to God;
In heaven are kept their grateful vows,
Their dust endears the sod.

Here holy thoughts a light have shed
From many a radiant face,
And prayers of humble virtue spread
The perfume of the place.

And anxious hearts have pondered here
The mystery of life,
And prayed th' Eternal Light to clear
Their doubts and aid their strife.

They live with God, their homes are dust;
Yet here their children pray,
And in this fleeting life-time trust
To find the narrow way.

Ralph Waldo Emerson

THE EIGHTY-FOURTH PSALM

How amiable are thy tabernacles, O Lord of hosts!
My soul longeth, yea, even fainteth
    for the courts of the Lord:
        my heart and my flesh crieth out for the living God.
Yea, the sparrow hath found an house,
    and the swallow a nest for herself,
        where she may lay her young,
            even thine altars, O Lord of hosts,
                my King and my God.
Blessed are they that dwell in thy house:
    they will be still praising thee.

Selah.

Blessed is the man whose strength is in thee:
    in whose heart are the ways of them:
Who passing through the valley of Baca, make it a well:
    the rain also filleth the pools.
They go from strength to strength:
    every one of them in Zion appeareth before God.
O Lord God of hosts, hear my prayer:
    give ear, O God of Jacob.

                                          Selah.

Behold, O God our shield:
    and look upon the face of thine anointed.
For a day in thy courts,
    is better than a thousand:
      I had rather be a doorkeeper
        in the house of my God,
            than to dwell in the tents of wickedness.
For the Lord God is a sun and shield:
    the Lord will give grace and glory:
      no good thing will he withhold
        from them that walk uprightly.
O Lord of hosts:
    blessed is the man that trusteth in thee.

FROM *HOLES IN THE SKY*

And man is a spirit
    And symbols are his meat,
So pull not down the steeple
    In your monied street.

For money chimes feebly,
    Matter dare not sing—
Man is a spirit,
    Let the bells ring.

Louis MacNeice

THOU, WHOSE UNMEASURED TEMPLE STANDS

Thou, whose unmeasured temple stands,
Built over earth and sea,
Accept the walls that human hands
Have raised, O God, to Thee.

And let the Comforter and Friend,
Thy Holy Spirit, meet
With those who here in worship bend
Before Thy mercy seat.

May they who err be guided here
To find the better way;
And they who mourn, and they who fear,
Be strengthened as they pray.

May faith grow firm, and love grow warm,
And pure devotion rise,
While round these hallowed walls the storm
Of earth-born passion dies.

William Cullen Bryant

IN HOC SIGNO

The Kingdoms of the Earth go by
   In purple and in gold;
They rise, they triumph, and they die,
   And all their tale is told.

One Kingdom only is divine,
   One banner triumphs still;
Its King a servant, and its sign
   A gibbet on a hill.

Godfrey Fox Bradby

FROM *THE CHURCH PORCH*

Let vain or busy thoughts have there no part;
Bring not thy plough, thy plots, thy pleasures thither.
Christ purged His Temple; so must thou thy heart:
All worldly thoughts are but thieves met together
    To cozen thee. Look to thy actions well;
      For churches either are our Heaven or Hell.

Judge not the preacher, for he is thy judge;
If thou mislike him, thou conceiv'st him not.
God calleth preaching folly: do not grudge
To pick out treasures from an earthen pot.
    The worst speak something good; if all want sense,
      God takes a text, and preacheth patience.

George Herbert

THE CHURCH IN THE HEART

Who builds a church within his heart
And takes it with him everywhere
Is holier far than he whose church
Is but a one-day house of prayer.

Morris Abel Beer

SEND FORTH, O GOD, THY LIGHT AND TRUTH

Send forth, O God, Thy light and truth,
And let them lead me still,
Undaunted, in the paths of right,
Up to Thy holy hill:
Then to Thy altar will I spring,
And in my God rejoice;
And praise shall tune the trembling string,
And gratitude my voice.

John Quincy Adams

ONE IN CHRIST

No form of human framing,
　　No bond of outward might,
Can bind Thy Church together, Lord,
　　And all her flocks unite;
But, Jesus, Thou hast told us
　　How unity must be:
Thou art with God the Father one,
　　And we are one in Thee.

The mind that is in Jesus
　　Will guide us into truth,
The humble, open, joyful mind
　　Of ever-learning youth;
The heart that is in Jesus
　　Will lead us out of strife,
The giving and forgiving heart
　　That follows love in life.

Wherever men adore Thee,
　　Our souls with them would kneel;
Wherever men implore Thy help,
　　Their trouble we would feel;
And where men do Thy service,
　　Though knowing not Thy sign,
Our hand is with them in good work,
　　For they are also Thine.

Forgive us, Lord, the folly
　　That quarrels with Thy friends,
And draws us nearer to Thy heart
　　Where every discord ends;
Thou art the crown of manhood,
　　And Thou of God the Son;
O Master of our many lives,
　　In Thee our life is one.

Henry van Dyke

289

CITY OF GOD

City of God, how broad and far
  Outspread thy walls sublime!
The true thy chartered freemen are,
  Of every age and clime.

How gleam thy watch fires through the night,
  With never-fainting ray!
How rise thy towers, serene and bright,
  To meet the dawning day!

In vain the surge's angry shock,
  In vain the drifting sands;
Unharmed upon the eternal rock
  The eternal city stands.

Samuel Johnson

THE ONE HUNDRED AND TWENTY-SECOND PSALM

I was glad when they said unto me,
Let us go into the house of the Lord.
Our feet shall stand within thy gates, O Jerusalem.
Jerusalem is builded as a city that is compact together:
Whither the tribes go up, the tribes of the Lord,
Unto the testimony of Israel,
To give thanks unto the name of the Lord.
For there are set thrones of judgment,
The thrones of the house of David.
Pray for the peace of Jerusalem:
They shall prosper that love thee.
Peace be within thy walls,
And prosperity within thy palaces.
For my brethren and companions' sakes, I will now say,
Peace be within thee.
Because of the house of the Lord our God
I will seek thy good.

29. The Ministry

I say the pulpit (in the sober use
Of its legitimate, peculiar pow'rs)
Must stand acknowledg'd, while the world shall stand,
The most important and effectual guard,
Support, and ornament, of virtue's cause.
There stands the messenger of truth: there stands
The legate of the skies!—His theme divine,
His office sacred, his credentials clear.
By him the violated law speaks out
Its thunders; and by him, in strains as sweet
As angels use, the gospel whispers peace.
He 'stablishes the strong, restores the weak,
Reclaims the wand'rer, binds the broken heart,
And, arm'd himself in panoply complete
Of heav'nly temper, furnishes with arms,
Bright as his own, and trains, by ev'ry rule
Of holy discipline, to glorious war,
The sacramental host of God's elect!

William Cowper

FROM *LOVE BREATHING THANKS AND PRAISE*

I preached as never sure to preach again,
And as a dying man to dying men.

Richard Baxter

from *THE CANTERBURY TALES*

The parson of a country town was he
Who knew the straits of humble poverty;
But rich he was in holy thought and work,
Nor less in learning as became a clerk.
The word of Christ most truly did he preach,
And his parishioners devoutly teach.
Benign was he, in labours diligent,
And in adversity was still content—
As proved full oft. To all his flock a friend,
Averse was he to ban or to contend
When tithes were due. Much rather was he fond,
Unto his poor parishioners around,
Of his own substance and his dues to give,
Content on little, for himself to live.
Wide was his parish, scattered far asunder,
Yet none did he neglect, in rain, or thunder.
Sorrow and sickness won his kindly care;
With staff in hand he travelled everywhere.
This good example to his sheep he brought
That first he wrought, and afterwards he taught.
This parable he joined the Word unto—
That, "If gold rust, what shall iron do?"
For if a priest be foul in whom we trust,
No wonder if a common man should rust!
And shame it were, in those the flock who keep
For shepherds to be foul yet clean the sheep.
Well ought a priest example fair to give,
By his own cleanness, how his sheep should live.
He did not put his benefice to hire,
And leave his sheep encumbered in the mire,
Then haste to St. Paul's in London Town,
To seek a chantry where to settle down,
And there at least to sing the daily mass,
Or with a brotherhood his time to pass.
He dwelt at home, with watchful care to keep

From prowling wolves his well-protected sheep.
Though holy in himself and virtuous
He still to sinful men was piteous,
Not sparing of his speech, in vain conceit,
But in his teaching kindly and discreet.
To draw his flock to heaven with noble art,
By good example, was his holy art.
Nor less did he rebuke the obstinate,
Whether they were of high or low estate.
For pomp and worldly show he did not care;
No morbid conscience made his rule severe.
The lore of Christ and his apostles twelve
He taught, but first he followed it himself.

Geoffrey Chaucer (translated by H. C. Leonard)

THE PRIEST OF CHRIST

Give me the priest these graces shall possess;
Of an ambassador the just address,
A Father's tenderness, a Shepherd's care,
A Leader's courage, which the cross can bear,
A Ruler's arm, a Watchman's wakeful eye,
A Pilot's skill, the helm in storms to ply,
A Fisher's patience, and a Labourer's toil,
A Guide's dexterity to disembroil,
A Prophet's inspiration from above,
A Teacher's knowledge, and a Saviour's love.
Give me a priest, a light upon a hill,
Whose rays his whole circumference can fill,
In God's own Word and Sacred Learning verse,
Deep in the study of the heart immersed,
Who in such souls can the disease descry,
And wisely fair restoratives supply.

Thomas Ken

EPITAPH ON A WORTHY CLERGYMAN

Still like his Master, known by breaking bread,
The good he entertained, the needy fed;
Of humour easy, and of life unblam'd,
The Friend delighted, while the Priest reclaim'd.
The Friend, the Father, and the Husband gone,
The Priest still lives in this recording stone;
Where pious eyes may read his praises o'er,
And learn each grace his pulpit taught before.

Benjamin Frankli

FROM *THE DESERTED VILLAGE*

Near yonder copse, where once the garden smiled,
And still where many a garden-flower grows wild,
There, where a few torn shrubs the place disclose,
The village preacher's modest mansion rose.
A man he was to all the country dear,
And passing rich with forty pounds a year.
Remote from towns he ran his godly race,
Nor e'er had changed, nor wish'd to change, his place;
Unskilful he to fawn, or seek for power
By doctrines fashion'd to the varying hour;
Far other aims his heart had learn'd to prize,
More bent to raise the wretched than to rise.
His house was known to all the vagrant train;
He chid their wanderings, but relieved their pain;
The long-remember'd beggar was his guest,
Whose beard descending swept his aged breast;
The ruin'd spendthrift, now no longer proud,
Claim'd kindred there, and had his claims allow'd;
The broken soldier, kindly bid to stay,
Sat by his fire, and talk'd the night away;—
Wept o'er his wounds, or, tales of sorrow done,
Shoulder'd his crutch, and show'd how fields were won.

Pleased with his guests, the good man learn'd to glow,
And quite forgot their vices in their woe;
Careless their merits or their faults to scan,
His pity gave ere charity began.
  Thus to relieve the wretched was his pride,
And even his failings lean'd to virtue's side;
But in his duty prompt at every call,
He watch'd and wept, he pray'd and felt for all:
And, as a bird each fond endearment tries,
To tempt its new-fledged offspring to the skies,
He tried each art, reproved each dull delay,
Allured to brighter worlds, and led the way.
  Beside the bed where parting life was laid,
And sorrow, guilt, and pain, by turns dismay'd,
The reverend champion stood. At his control,
Despair and anguish fled the struggling soul;
Comfort came down the trembling wretch to raise,
And his last faltering accents whisper'd praise.
  At church, with meek and unaffected grace,
His looks adorn'd the venerable place;
Truth from his lips prevail'd with double sway,
And fools, who came to scoff, remain'd to pray.
The service past, around the pious man
With steady zeal, each honest rustic ran;
E'en children follow'd, with endearing wile,
And pluck'd his gown, to share the good man's smile;
His ready smile a parent's warmth express'd;
Their welfare pleased him, and their cares distress'd;
To them his heart, his love, his griefs were given
But all his serious thoughts had rest in heaven.
As some tall cliff that lifts its awful form,
Swells from the vale, and midway leaves the storm,
Though round its breast the rolling clouds are spread,
Eternal sunshine settles on its head.

Oliver Goldsmith

THE PREACHER'S PRAYER

If thou wouldst have me speak, Lord, give me speech.
So many cries are uttered nowadays,
That scarce a song, however clear and true,
Will thread the jostling tumult safe, and reach
The ears of men buz-filled with poor denays:
Barb thou my words with light, make my song new,
And men will hear, or when I sing or preach.

George Macdonald

FROM *THE TASK*

Would I describe a preacher, such as Paul,
Were he on earth, would hear, approve, and own—
Paul should himself direct me. I would trace
His master-strokes, and draw from his design.
I would express him simple, grave, sincere;
In doctrine uncorrupt; in language plain,
And plain in manner; decent, solemn, chaste,
And natural in gesture; much impressed
Himself, as conscious of his awful charge,
And anxious mainly that the flock he feeds
May feel it too; affectionate in look,
And tender in address, as well becomes
A messenger of grace to guilty men.
Behold the picture!—Is it like?—Like whom?
The things that mount the rostrum with a skip,
And then skip down again; pronounce a text;
Cry—hem! and reading what they never wrote,
Just fifteen minutes, huddle up their work,
And with a well-bred whisper close the scene!

William Cowper

THE HAND THAT HELD IT

He held the lamp of Truth that day
So low that none could miss the way;
And yet so high to bring in sight
That picture fair—the World's Great Light—
That gazing up (the lamp between)
The hand that held it scarce was seen.

W. G. Elmslie

FROM THE RUBÁIYÁT OF OMAR KHAYYÁM

Why, all the Saints and Sages who discuss'd
Of the Two Worlds so learnedly are thrust
    Like foolish Prophets forth; their Words to Scorn
Are scatter'd, and their Mouths are stopt with Dust.

Myself when young did eagerly frequent
Doctor and Saint, and heard great argument
    About it and about: but evermore
Came out by the same door as in I went.

With them the seed of Wisdom did I sow,
And with my own hand wrought to make it grow;
    And this was all the Harvest that I reap'd—
"I came like Water, and like Wind I go."

Edward FitzGerald

THE ONE HUNDRED AND THIRTY-FOURTH PSALM

Behold, bless ye the Lord,
All ye servants of the Lord,
Which by night stand in the house of the Lord.
Lift up your hands in the sanctuary,
And bless the Lord.
The Lord that made heaven and earth
Bless thee out of Zion.

30. Social Concern

TURN BACK, O MAN

Turn back, O man, forswear thy foolish ways.
Old now is Earth, and none may count her days,
Yet thou, her child, whose head is crowned with flame,
Still wilt not hear thine inner God proclaim—
"Turn back, O man, forswear thy foolish ways."

Earth might be fair and all men glad and wise.
Age after age their tragic empires rise,
Built while they dream, and in that dreaming weep:
Would man but wake from out his haunted sleep,
Earth might be fair and all men glad and wise.

Earth shall be fair, and all her people one:
Nor till that hour shall God's whole will be done.
Now, even now, once more from earth to sky,
Peals forth in joy man's old, undaunted cry—
"Earth shall be fair, and all her folk be one!"

Clifford Bax

"WHEN I THINK OF THE HUNGRY PEOPLE"

I have a suit of new clothes in this happy new year;
    Hot rice cake soup is excellent to my taste;
But when I think of the hungry people in this city,
    I am ashamed of my fortune in the presence of God.

O-Shi-O (Japanese scholar)

LOVE

My God is Love;
My God is Love,
Tender and deep;
I feel His close, sweet presence
Looking down to see
The beggar-baby
Lying in my arms asleep.

Toyohiko Kagawa

MIDNIGHT

God help the homeless ones who lack this night
A roof for shelter and a couch for sleep;
God help the sailormen who long for light
As restlessly they toss upon the deep.

God keep the orphaned children who are left
Unmothered in this world of chill and dole;
God keep the widowed hearts, of joy bereft;
God make all weary broken spirits whole.

Dark broods the midnight over sea and land,
No star illumes the blackness of the sky.
But safe as nested birds within Thy hand,
God of our Fathers, we Thy children lie.

Margaret E. Sangster

A LADY I KNOW

She thinks that even up in heaven
Her class lies late and snores,
While poor black cherubs rise at seven
To do celestial chores.

Countee Cullen

FROM *THE POSTERN GATE*

In the castle of my soul
Is a little postern gate,
Whereat, when I enter,
    I am in the presence of God.
In a moment, in the turning of a thought,
I am where God is.
This is a fact.

This world of ours has length and breadth,
A superficial and horizontal world.
When I am with God
I look deep down and high up,
And all is changed.
The world of men is made of jangling noises.
With God is a great silence.
But that silence is a melody
Sweet as the contentment of love,
Thrilling as a touch of flame.

In this world my days are few
And full of trouble.
I strive and have not;
I seek and find not;
I ask and learn not.
Its joys are so fleeting,
Its pains are so enduring,
I am in doubt if life be worth living.
When I enter into God,
All life has a meaning.

Without asking I know;
My desires are even now fulfilled,
My fever is gone
In the great quiet of God.
My troubles are but pebbles on the road,
My joys are like the everlasting hills.

So it is when I step through the gate of prayer
From time into eternity
When I am in the consciousness of God,
My fellowmen are not far-off and forgotten,
But close and strangely dear.

*   *   *

Big things become small, and small things become great.
The near becomes far, and the future is near.
The lowly and despised is shot through with glory,
And most of human power and greatness
Seems as full of infernal iniquities
As a carcass is full of maggots.
God is the substance of all revolutions;
When I am in him, I am in the Kingdom of God
And in the Fatherland of my Soul.

Walter Rauschenbusch

WE ARE LIVING, WE ARE DWELLING

We are living, we are dwelling
    In a grand and awful time,
In an age on ages telling;
    To be living is sublime.
Hark! the waking up of nations,
    Hosts advancing to the fray;
Hark! what soundeth is creation's
    Groaning for the latter day.

Will ye play, then? will ye dally
    Far behind the battle line?
Up! it is Jehovah's rally;
    God's own arm hath need of thine.
Worlds are charging, heaven beholding;
    Thou hast but an hour to fight;
Now, the blazoned cross unfolding,
    On, right onward for the right!

Sworn to yield, to waver, never,
    Consecrated, born again,
Sworn to be Christ's soldiers ever,
    O for Christ at least be men!
O let all the soul within you
    For the truth's sake go abroad!
Strike! let every blaze and sinew
    Tell on ages, tell for God.

Arthur C. Coxe

FROM *IN MEMORIAM*

Ring out, wild bells, to the wild sky,
    The flying cloud, the frosty light:
    The year is dying in the night;
Ring out, wild bells, and let him die.

Ring out a slowly dying cause,
    And ancient forms of party strife;
    Ring in the nobler modes of life,
With sweeter manners, purer laws.

Ring out false pride in place and blood,
    The civic slander and the spite;
    Ring in the love of truth and right,
Ring in the common love of good.

Ring out old shapes of foul disease;
    Ring out the narrowing lust of gold;
    Ring out the thousand wars of old,
Ring in the thousand years of peace.

Ring in the valiant man and free,
    The larger heart, the kindlier hand:
    Ring out the darkness of the land,
Ring in the Christ that is to be.

Alfred Tennyson

FROM *THE VISION OF SIR LAUNFAL*

"The Holy Supper is kept, indeed,
In whatso we share with another's need;
Not what we give, but what we share,
For the gift without the giver is bare;
Who gives himself with his alms feeds three,
Himself, his hungering neighbor, and Me."

James Russell Lowell

THE WAY, THE TRUTH, AND THE LIFE

O thou great Friend to all the sons of men,
Who once appear'dst in humblest guise below,
Sin to rebuke, to break the captive's chain,
To call thy brethren forth from want and woe!—
Thee would I sing. Thy truth is still the light
Which guides the nations groping on their way,
Stumbling and falling in disastrous night,
Yet hoping ever for the perfect day.
Yes, thou art still the life; thou art the way
The holiest know,—light, life, and way of heaven;
And they who dearest hope and deepest pray
Toil by the truth, life, way that thou hast given;
And in thy name aspiring mortals trust
To uplift their bleeding brothers rescued from the dust.

Theodore Parker

FROM *THE TAO TEH KING*

The slaying of multitudes should be mourned with sorrow.
A victory should be celebrated with the Funeral Rite.

Author unknown (Chinese)

303

ULTIMATUM

Now the frontiers are all closed.
There is no other country we can run away to.
There is no ocean we can cross over.
At last we must turn and live with one another.

We cannot escape this day any longer.
We cannot continue to choose between good and evil
    (the good for ourselves, the evil for our neighbors);
We must all bear the equal burden.

At last we who have been running away must turn and face it.
There is no room for hate left in the world we must live in.
Now we must learn love. We can no longer escape it.
We can no longer escape from one another.

Love is no longer a theme for eloquence, or a way of life
    for a few to choose whose hearts can decide it.
It is the sternest necessity; the unequivocal ultimatum.
There is no other way out; there is no country we can flee to.
There is no man on earth who must not face this task now.

Peggy Pond Church

FROM *THE OXYRHYNCUS SAYINGS OF JESUS*

Lift up the stone, and there thou shalt find Me:
Cleave the wood, and I am there.

THEY WHO TREAD THE PATH OF LABOR

They who tread the path of labor
    follow where My feet have trod;
They who work without complaining
    do the holy will of God;

304

Where the many toil together,
    there am I among My own;
Where the tired workman sleepeth,
    there am I with him alone.

I, the peace that passeth knowledge,
    dwell amid the daily strife;
I, the bread of heaven, am broken
    in the sacrament of life.

Every task, however simple,
    sets the soul that does it free;
Every deed of love and mercy,
    done to man, is done to Me.

        *   *   *

Nevermore thou needest seek Me;
    I am with thee everywhere;
Raise the stone, and thou shalt find Me;
    cleave the wood, and I am there.

                      Henry van Dyke

BEFORE THY THRONE

Before Thy throne, O God, we kneel;
    Give us a conscience quick to feel,
A ready mind to understand
    The meaning of Thy chastening hand;
Whate'er the pain and shame may be,
Bring us, O Father, nearer Thee.

Search out our hearts and make us true,
    Wishful to give to all their due;
From love of pleasure, lust of gold,
    From sins which make the heart grow cold,
Wean us and train us with Thy rod;
Teach us to know our faults, O God.

For sins of heedless word and deed,
   For pride ambitious to succeed;
For crafty trade and subtle snare
   To catch the simple unaware;
For lives bereft of purpose high,
Forgive, forgive, O Lord, we cry.

Let the fierce fires, which burn and try,
   Our inmost spirits purify:
Consume the ill; purge out the shame;
   O God! be with us in the flame;
A newborn people may we rise,
More pure, more true, more nobly wise.

William Boyd Carpenter

O, MAY I JOIN THE CHOIR INVISIBLE!

O, may I join the choir invisible
Of those immortal dead who live again
In minds made better by their presence; live
In pulses stirred to generosity,
In deeds of daring rectitude, in scorn
Of miserable aims that end with self,
In thoughts sublime that pierce the night like stars,
And with their mild persistence urge men's minds
To vaster issues.
        So to live is heaven:
To make undying music in the world,
Breathing a beauteous order, that controls
With growing sway the growing life of man. . . .
           May I reach
That purest heaven,—be to other souls
The cup of strength in some great agony,
Enkindle generous ardor, feed pure love,

Beget the smiles that have no cruelty,
Be the sweet presence of a good diffused,
And in diffusion ever more intense!
So shall I join the choir invisible,
Whose music is the gladness of the world.

George Eliot

THE LORD'S PRAYER

Our Father, who art in heaven,
    Hallowed be Thy name.
    Thy Kingdom come.
    Thy will be done on earth
        as it is in heaven.
Give us this day our daily bread.
And forgive us our debts,
    as we forgive our debtors.
And lead us not into temptation,
    but deliver us from evil:
For Thine is the Kingdom,
    and the power,
    and the glory,
        for ever. Amen.

Jesus (Matthew 6:9-13)

THE LATEST DECALOGUE

Thou shalt have one God only; who
Would be at the expense of two?
No graven images may be
Worshipped, except the currency:
Swear not at all; for, for thy curse
Thine enemy is none the worse:
At church on Sunday to attend
Will serve to keep the world thy friend:

Honour thy parents; that is, all
From whom advancement may befall:
Thou shalt not kill; but needst not strive
Officiously to keep alive:
Do not adultery commit;
Advantage rarely comes of it:
Thou shalt not steal; an empty feat,
When it's so lucrative to cheat:
Bear not false witness; let the lie
Have time on its own wings to fly:
Thou shalt not covet; but tradition
Approves all forms of competition.
The sum of all is, thou shalt love,
If any body, God above:
At any rate shall never labour
More than thyself to love thy neighbour.

Arthur Hugh Clough

RIGHT IS RIGHT

For right is right, since God is God,
    And right the day must win;
To doubt would be disloyalty,
    To falter would be sin.

Frederick W. Faber

FROM *SACRIFICE*

Though love repine, and reason chafe,
    There came a voice without reply,—
" 'Tis man's perdition to be safe,
    When for the truth he ought to die."

Ralph Waldo Emerson

308

THE SEARCH

I went to seek for Christ,
  And Nature seemed so fair
That first the woods and fields my youth enticed,
  And I was sure to find him there:
    The temple I forsook,
    And to the solitude
Allegiance paid; but Winter came and shook
  The crown and purple from my wood;
His snows, like desert sands, with scornful drift,
  Besieged the columned aisle and palace-gate;
My Thebes, cut deep with many a solemn rift,
  But epitaphed her own sepulchred state:
Then I remembered whom I went to seek,
And blessed blunt Winter for his counsel bleak.

    Back to the world I turned,
    For Christ, I said, is King;
So the cramped alley and the hut I spurned,
    As far beneath his sojourning:
      'Mid power and wealth I sought,
      But found no trace of him,
And all the costly offerings I had brought
    With sudden rust and mould grew dim:
I found his tomb, indeed, where, by their laws,
    All must on stated days themselves imprison,
Mocking with bread a dead creed's grinning jaws,
    Witless how long the life had thence arisen;
Due sacrifice to this they set apart,
Prizing it more than Christ's own living heart.

      So from my feet the dust
      Of the proud World I shook;
Then came dear Love and shared with me his crust,
      And half my sorrow's burden took.
        After the World's soft bed,
        Its rich and dainty fare,

Like down seemed Love's coarse pillow to my head
   His cheap food seemed as manna rare;
Fresh-trodden prints of bare and bleeding feet,
   Turned to the heedless city whence I came,
Hard by I saw, and springs of worship sweet
   Gushed from my cleft heart smitten by the same;
Love looked me in the face and spake no words,
But straight I knew those footprints were the Lord's.

     I followed where they led
     And in a hovel rude,
With naught to fence the weather from his head,
   The King I sought for meekly stood;
     A naked, hungry child
     Clung round his gracious knee,
And a poor hunted slave looked up and smiled
   To bless the smile that set him free;
New miracles I saw his presence do,—
   No more I knew the hovel bare and poor,
The gathered chips into a woodpile grew,
   The broken morsel swelled to goodly store;
I knelt and wept: my Christ no more I seek,
His throne is with the outcast and the weak.

                James Russell Lowell

THE FATHER'S BUSINESS

Who puts back into place a fallen bar,
   Or flings a rock out of a traveled road,
His feet are moving toward the central star,
   His name is whispered in the God's abode.

                Edwin Markham

31. *Justice and Righteousness*

WANTED

God give us men! A time like this demands
Strong minds, great hearts, true faith, and ready hands;
Men whom the lust of office does not kill;
   Men whom the spoils of office cannot buy;
Men who possess opinions and a will;
   Men who have honor,—men who will not lie;
Men who can stand before a demagogue,
   And damn his treacherous flatteries without winking!
Tall men, sun-crowned, who live above the fog
   In public duty, and in private thinking:
For while the rabble, with their thumb-worn creeds,
Their large professions and their little deeds,—
Mingle in selfish strife, lo! Freedom weeps,
Wrong rules the land, and waiting Justice sleeps.

J. G. Holland

I AM NOT BOUND TO WIN

I am not bound to win,
But I am bound to be true.
I am not bound to succeed,
But I am bound to live up to what light I have.
I must stand with anybody that stands right;
Stand with him while he is right,
And part with him when he goes wrong.

Abraham Lincoln

311

SLAVES

They are slaves who fear to speak,
    For the fallen and the weak;
They are slaves who will not choose,
    Hatred, scoffing and abuse;
Rather than in silence shrink,
    From the truth they needs must think;
They are slaves who dare not be
    In the right with two or three.

James Russell Lowell

SAID THE INNKEEPER

I cannot take these poor;
They do not pay;
They brand the house, they bring disgrace;
I had to send that pair away . . .
And yet there was a strange look on her face,
This girl who kept her eyes upon the floor,
So strange I stopped a space
Before I sent them from the door.

What could I do?
A man must make a living while he may,
And trade is trade, and money, too,
And sentiment is not, I say.

And yet this girl was strangely fair:
She shivered in the doorway there,
And once she raised her eyes to mine . . .
I bowed; I would have knelt, I swear,
But at the table some poor lout
Made cry for wine
And broke the spell . . .

I saw the poorness of the pair
And put them out.
And I did well.
Two merchants took the great room overhead.
It is my principle: I buy and sell
And give my pity to the dead.

And yet this girl, this girl . . .
I turned her from my door,
But she looked back with kindly eyes
And fairer than before,
And went away
As if she walked with emperors
And was a queen, and all the world was hers!

What could I say?
A man must make his living while he may.

Myles Connolly

WHEREWITH SHALL I COME BEFORE THE LORD?

Wherewith shall I come before the Lord,
    and bow myself before the high God?
        shall I come before him with burnt offerings,
            with calves of a year old?
Will the Lord be pleased with thousands of rams,
    or with ten thousands of rivers of oil?
        shall I give my firstborn for my transgression,
            the fruit of my body for the sin of my soul?
He hath showed thee, O man, what is good;
    and what doth the Lord require of thee,
        but to do justly,
            and to love mercy,
                and to walk humbly with thy God?

Micah the Prophet (Micah 6:6-8)

A FREE NATION

And this freedom will be the freedom of all.
It will loosen both master and slave from the chain.
For, by a divine paradox,
Wherever there is one slave
There are two.
So in the wonderful reciprocities of being,
We can never reach the higher levels
Until all our fellows ascend with us.
There is no true liberty for the individual
Except as he finds it
In the liberty of all.
There is no true security for the individual
Except as he finds it
In the security of all.

Edwin Markham

FOUNDATIONS

Those things which cannot be shaken.—HEBREWS 12:28

Now again the world is shaken,
   Tempests break on sea and shore;
Earth with ruin overtaken,
   Trembles while the storm-winds roar.
      He abideth who confideth,
God is God forevermore.

Thrones are falling, heathen raging,
   Peoples dreaming as of yore
Vain imaginations, waging
   Man with man, unmeaning war.
      He abideth who confideth,
Christ is King forevermore.

Human wisdom in confusion,
　　Casts away the forms it wore;
Ancient error, new illusion,
　　Lose the phantom fruit they bore.
　　　　He abideth who confideth,
Truth is truth forevermore.

Right eternal, Love immortal,
　　Built the House where we adore;
Mercy is its golden portal,
　　Virtue its unshaken floor.
　　　　He abideth who confideth,
God is God forevermore.

Henry van Dyke

LATIMER'S LIGHT

In Oxford town the faggots they piled,
With furious haste and curses wild,
Round two brave men of our British breed,
Who dared to stand true to their speech and deed;
Round two brave men of that sturdy race,
Who with tremorless souls the worst can face;
Round two brave souls who could keep their tryst
Through a pathway of fire to follow Christ.
And the flames leaped up, but the blinding smoke
Could not the soul of Hugh Latimer choke;
For, said he, "Brother Ridley, be of good cheer,
A candle in England is lighted here,
Which by grace of God shall never go out,—"
And that speech in whispers was echoed about,—
　　Latimer's Light shall never go out,
　　However the winds may blow it about;
　　Latimer's Light is here to stay
　　Till the trump of a coming judgment day.

Author unknown

315

FROM *THE PRESENT CRISIS*

Careless seems the great Avenger; history's pages but record
One death-struggle in the darkness 'twixt old systems and the Word;
Truth forever on the scaffold, Wrong forever on the throne,—
Yet that scaffold sways the future, and, behind the dim unknown,
Standeth God within the shadow, keeping watch above His own.

James Russell Lowell

FOUR THINGS

Four things a man must learn to do
If he would make his record true:
To think without confusion clearly;
To love his fellowmen sincerely;
To act from honest motives purely;
To trust in God and Heaven securely.

Henry van Dyke

THE CENTURIES ARE HIS

The centuries are His. I will not be
   Dismayed when evil men and days prevail,
Though God may seem to be on Calvary,
   And peace may walk alone a midnight trail.

God does not balance books along the way,
   Yet always there will be a judgment day.
The centuries are His and He is just;
   His Kingdom shall yet rule though stars be dust.

Georgia Moore Eberling

316

32. Brotherhood and World Peace

IF WE BREAK FAITH—

When they write an end to war, when they blot away the battle,
While our hearts are hushed in thankfulness and prayer,
With the signatures still wet, Lord, let us not forget
The ghostly line who also sign, though no one sees them there.

They crowd into that railroad car, they throng that flagship's cabin—
The ghosts of all the dead men in long unending lines:
From the hell-defended rock, from the hallowed beachhead flock
The dead who stand and grip his hand each time the signer signs.

If we break faith with these our dead, play fast and loose with honor:
If we once more betray them as we have betrayed them twice,
We have earned their bitter curse that shall blast the universe . . .
Judge Thou us then, O Judge of men, if we deny them thrice!

Joseph Auslander

O BROTHER MAN

O brother man, fold to thy heart thy brother
Where pity dwells, the peace of God is there;
To worship rightly is to love each other,
Each smile a hymn, each kindly deed a prayer.

Follow with reverent steps the great example
Of Him whose holy work was doing good:
So shall the wide earth seem our Father's temple,
Each loving life a psalm of gratitude.

Then shall all shackles fall; the stormy clangor
Of wild war-music o'er the earth shall cease;
Love shall tread out the baleful fire of anger,
And in its ashes plant the tree of peace.

John Greenleaf Whittier

A SIGHT IN CAMP

A sight in camp in the daybreak gray and dim,
As from my tent I emerge so early sleepless,
As slow I walk in the cool fresh air the path near by the hospital
    tent.
Three forms I see on stretchers lying, brought out there untended
    lying,
Over each the blanket spread, ample brownish woolen blanket,
Gray and heavy blanket, folding, covering all.
Curious I halt and silent stand,
Then with light fingers I from the face of the nearest the first just
    lift the blanket;
Who are you elderly man so gaunt and grim, with well-gray'd hair,
    and flesh all sunken about the eyes?
Who are you my dear comrade?

Then to the second I step—and who are you my child and darling?
Who are you sweet boy with cheeks yet blooming?

Then to the third—a face nor child nor old, very calm, as of
    beautiful yellow-white ivory;
Young man I think I know you—I think this face is the face of the
    Christ himself,
Dead and divine and brother of all, and here again he lies.

Walt Whitman

318

FROM *THE OVER-HEART*

The world sits at the feet of Christ,
 Unknowing, blind and unconsoled;
  It yet shall touch His garment's fold,
And feel the heavenly Alchemist
 Transform its very dust to gold.

John Greenleaf Whittier

FROM *LOCKSLEY HALL*

For I dipt into the future, far as human eye could see,
Saw the Vision of the world, and all the wonder that would be;

Saw the heavens fill with commerce, argosies of magic sails,
Pilots of the purple twilight, dropping down with costly bales;

Heard the heavens fill with shouting, and there rain'd a ghastly dew
From the nations' airy navies grappling in the central blue;

Far along the world-wide whisper of the south-wind rushing warm,
With the standards of the peoples plunging thro' the thunder-storm;

Till the war-drum throbb'd no longer, and the battle-flags were
 furl'd
In the Parliament of man, the Federation of the world.

There the common sense of most shall hold a fretful realm in awe,
And the kindly earth shall slumber, lapt in universal law.

Alfred Tennyson

CHRISTMAS BELLS

I heard the bells on Christmas Day
 Their old, familiar carols play,
  And wild and sweet

319

The words repeat
Of peace on earth, good will to men!

And thought how, as the day had come,
The belfries of all Christendom
    Had rolled along
    The unbroken song
Of peace on earth, good will to men!

Till, ringing, singing on its way,
The world revolved from night to day,
    A voice, a chime,
    A chant sublime
Of peace on earth, good will to men!

Then from each black, accursed mouth
The cannon thundered in the South,
    And with the sound
    The carols drowned
Of peace on earth, good will to men!

It was as if an earthquake rent
The hearthstones of a continent,
    And made forlorn
    The households born
Of peace on earth, good will to men!

And in despair I bowed my head;
"There is no peace on earth," I said;
    "For hate is strong,
    And mocks the song
Of peace on earth, good will to men!"

Then pealed the bells more loud and deep;
"God is not dead; nor doth he sleep!
    The wrong shall fail,
    The right prevail,
With peace on earth, good will to men!"

Henry Wadsworth Longfellow

NEITHER SHALL THEY LEARN WAR ANY MORE

But in the last days it shall come to pass,
That the mountain of the house of the Lord shall be established
   in the top of the mountains,
     and it shall be exalted above the hills;
       and people shall flow unto it.
And many nations shall come, and say,
  Come, and let us go up to the mountain of the Lord,
    and to the house of the God of Jacob;
  and he will teach us of his ways,
    and we will walk in his paths:
      for the law shall go forth from Jerusalem.
And he shall judge among many people,
  and rebuke strong nations afar off;
And they shall beat their swords into plowshares,
  and their spears into pruning hooks:
Nation shall not lift up a sword against nation,
  neither shall they learn war any more.
But they shall sit
  every man
    under his vine and under his fig tree;
     and none shall make them afraid:
For the mouth of the Lord of hosts hath spoken it.

Micah the Prophet (Micah 4:1-4)

FROM *BALLAD OF EAST AND WEST*

Oh, East is East, and West is West,
  and never the twain shall meet,
Till Earth and Sky stand presently at God's great Judgment Seat.
But there is neither East nor West, Border, nor Breed, nor Birth,
When two strong men stand face to face,
  though they come from the ends of the earth!

Rudyard Kipling
321

NO EAST OR WEST

In Christ there is no East or West,
    In Him no South or North,
But one great Fellowship of Love
    Throughout the whole wide earth.

In Him shall true hearts everywhere
    Their high communion find.
His service is the golden cord
    Close-binding all mankind.

Join hands then, Brothers of the Faith,
    Whate'er your race may be!—
Who serves my Father as a son
    Is surely kin to me.

In Christ now meet both East and West,
    In Him meet South and North,
All Christly souls are one in Him,
    Throughout the whole wide earth.

John Oxenham

FOR WHOM THE BELL TOLLS

Any man's death diminishes me
Because I am involved in Mankinde;
And therefore never send to know
For whom the bell tolls,
It tolls for thee.

John Donne

WE BEAR THE STRAIN OF EARTHLY CARE

We bear the strain of earthly care,
But bear it not alone.

Beside us walks our brother Christ,
And makes our task his own.

Through din of market, whirl of wheels,
And thrust of driving trade,
We follow where the Master leads,
Serene and unafraid.

The common hopes that make us men
Were his in Galilee;
The tasks he gives are those he gave
Beside the restless sea.

Our brotherhood still rests in him,
The brother of us all,
And o'er the centuries still we hear
The Master's winsome call.

Ozora S. Davis

AFTER BLENHEIM

It was a summer evening,
    Old Kaspar's work was done,
And he before his cottage door
    Was sitting in the sun;
And by him sported on the green
His little grandchild Wilhelmine.

She saw her brother Peterkin
    Roll something large and round
Which he beside the rivulet
    In playing there had found;
He came to ask what he had found
That was so large and smooth and round.

Old Kaspar took it from the boy
    Who stood expectant by;

And then the old man shook his head,
   And with a natural sigh
' 'Tis some poor fellow's skull,' said he,
'Who fell in the great victory.

'I find them in the garden,
   For there's many here about;
And often when I go to plough
   The ploughshare turns them out.
For many thousand men,' said he,
'Were slain in that great victory.'

'Now tell us what 'twas all about,'
   Young Peterkin he cries;
And little Wilhelmine looks up
   With wonder-waiting eyes;
'Now tell us all about the war,
And what they fought each other for.'

'It was the English,' Kaspar cried,
   'Who put the French to rout;
But what they fought each other for
   I could not well make out.
But every body said,' quoth he,
'That 'twas a famous victory.

'My father lived at Blenheim then,
   Yon little stream hard by;
They burnt his dwelling to the ground,
   And he was forced to fly:
So with his wife and child he fled,
Nor had he where to rest his head.

'With fire and sword the country round
   Was wasted far and wide,
And many a childing mother then
   And newborn baby died:

But things like that, you know, must be
At every famous victory.

'They say it was a shocking sight
   After the field was won;
For many thousand bodies here
   Lay rotting in the sun:
But things like that, you know, must be
After a famous victory.

'Great praise the Duke of Marlbro' won
   And our good Prince Eugene;'
'Why 'twas a very wicked thing!'
   Said little Wilhelmine;
'Nay . . . nay . . . my little girl,' quoth he,
'It was a famous victory.

'And every body praised the Duke
   Who this great fight did win.'
'But what good came of it at last?'
   Quoth little Peterkin:—
'Why that I cannot tell,' said he,
'But 'twas a famous victory.'

                   Robert Southey

APPARITIONS

Who goes there, in the night,
   Across the storm-swept plain?
We are the ghosts of a valiant war—
   A million murdered men!

Who goes there, at the dawn,
   Across the sun-swept plain?
We are the hosts of those who swear:
   It shall not be again!

               Thomas Curtis Clark

THESE THINGS SHALL BE

These things shall be: a loftier race
  Than e'er the world hath known shall rise
With flame of freedom in their souls,
  And light of knowledge in their eyes;

They shall be gentle, brave, and strong
  To spill no drop of blood, but dare
All that may plant man's lordship firm
  On earth and fire and sea and air;

Nation with nation, land with land,
  In-armed shall live as comrades free;
In every heart and brain shall throb
  The pulse of one fraternity;

There shall be no more sin, nor shame,
  Though pain and passion may not die,
For man shall be at one with God
  In bonds of firm necessity.

John A. Symonds

THE DIVINE IMAGE

To Mercy, Pity, Peace, and Love
All pray in their distress;
And to these virtues of delight
Return their thankfulness.

For Mercy, Pity, Peace, and Love
Is God, our father dear,
And Mercy, Pity, Peace, and Love
Is Man, his child and care.

For Mercy has a human heart,
Pity a human face,
And Love, the human form divine,
And Peace, the human dress.

Then every man, of every clime,
That prays in his distress,
Prays to the human form divine,
Love, Mercy, Pity, Peace.

And all must love the human form,
In heathen, Turk, or Jew;
Where Mercy, Love and Pity dwell,
There God is dwelling too.

William Blake

GOD'S RESIDENCE

Who has not found the heaven below
    Will fail of it above.
God's residence is next to mine—
    His furniture is love.

Emily Dickinson

TWO AT A FIRESIDE

I built a chimney for a comrade old;
    I did the service not for hope or hire:
And then I traveled on in winter's cold,
    Yet all the day I glowed before the fire.

Edwin Markham

33. *The Life Everlasting*

L'ENVOI

When earth's last picture is painted, and the tubes are twisted
 and dried,
When the oldest colors have faded,
 and the youngest critic has died,
We shall rest, and—faith, we shall need it,
 —lie down for an aeon or two,
Till the Master of all Good Workmen shall set us to work anew!

And those that were good shall be happy:
 they shall sit in a golden chair;
They shall splash at a ten-league canvas
 with brushes of comets' hair;
They shall find real saints to draw from—
 Magdalen, Peter, and Paul;
They shall work for an age at a sitting,
 and never be tired at all!

And only the Master shall praise us,
 and only the Master shall blame;
And no one shall work for money,
 and no one shall work for fame;
But each for the joy of the working,
 and each in his separate star
Shall draw the Thing as he sees It
 for the God of the Things as They are!

Rudyard Kipling

CROSSING THE BAR

Sunset and evening star,
   And one clear call for me!
And may there be no moaning of the bar,
   When I put out to sea,

But such a tide as moving seems asleep,
   Too full for sound and foam,
When that which drew from out the boundless deep
   Turns again home.

Twilight and evening bell,
   And after that the dark!
And may there be no sadness of farewell,
   When I embark;

For tho' from out our bourne of Time and Place
   The flood may bear me far,
I hope to see my Pilot face to face
   When I have crossed the bar.

Alfred Tennyson

FROM *LAST LINES*

Though earth and man were gone,
   And suns and universes cease to be,
   And Thou wert left alone,
Every existence would exist in Thee.

There is not room for Death,
   Nor atom that his might could render void:
   Thou—THOU art Being and Breath,
And what Thou art may never be destroyed.

Emily Brontë
329

SOME LATE LARK SINGING

A late lark twitters from the quiet skies:
And from the west,
Where the sun, his day's work ended,
Lingers as in content,
There falls on the old, gray city
An influence luminous and serene,
A shining peace.

The smoke ascends
In a rosy-and-golden haze. The spires
Shine and are changed. In the valley
Shadows rise. The lark sings on.
   The sun,
Closing his benediction,
Sinks, and the darkening air
Thrills with a sense of the triumphing night—
Night with her train of stars
And her great gift of sleep.

So be my passing!
My task accomplished and the long day done,
My wages taken, and in my heart
   Some late lark singing,
Let me be gathered to the quiet west,
The sundown splendid and serene,
   Death.

William Ernest Henley

FROM *THE OLD ASTRONOMER*

Though my soul may set in darkness, it will rise in perfect
   light,
I have loved the stars too fondly to be fearful of the
   night.

Sarah Williams

HOME AT LAST

To an open house in the evening,
Home shall men come,
To an older place than Eden,
And a taller town than Rome.
To the end of the way of the wandering star,
To the things that cannot be and are,
To the place where God was homeless,
And all men are at home.

G. K. Chesterton

ON TIME

Fly envious *Time*, till thou run out thy race,
Call on the lazy leaden-stepping hours,
Whose speed is but the heavy plummet's pace;
And glut thyself with what thy womb devours,
Which is no more than what is false and vain,
And merely mortal dross;
So little is our loss,
So little is thy gain.
For when as each thing bad thou hast entomb'd,
And last of all, thy greedy self consum'd,
Then long Eternity shall greet our bliss
With an individual kiss;
And joy shall overtake us as a flood,
When everything that is sincerely good
And perfectly divine,
With truth, and peace, and love shall ever shine
About the supreme Throne
Of him, t'whose happy-making sight alone,
When once our heav'nly-guided soul shall climb,
Then all this earthy grossness quit,
Attir'd with stars, we shall for ever sit,
Triumphing over death, and chance, and thee, O Time.

John Milton

THE SLEEP

He giveth his beloved sleep.—PSALM 127:2

Of all the thoughts of God that are
Borne inward unto souls afar,
Along the Psalmist's music deep,
Now tell me if that any is,
For gift or grace, surpassing this—
'He giveth His belovèd sleep'?

What would we give to our beloved?
The hero's heart to be unmoved,
The poet's star-tuned harp, to sweep,
The patriot's voice, to teach and rouse,
The monarch's crown, to light the brows?—
He giveth His belovèd, sleep.

What do we give to our beloved?
A little faith all undisproved,
A little dust to overweep,
And bitter memories to make
The whole earth blasted for our sake.
He giveth His belovèd, sleep.

'Sleep soft, beloved!' we sometimes say,
But have no tune to charm away
Sad dreams that through the eye-lids creep.
But never doleful dream again
Shall break the happy slumber when
He giveth His belovèd, sleep.

O earth, so full of dreary noises!
O men, with wailing in your voices!
O delvèd gold, the wailers heap!
O strife, O curse, that o'er it fall!
God strikes a silence through you all,
He giveth His belovèd, sleep.

His dews drop mutely on the hill;
His cloud above it saileth still,
Though on its slope men sow and reap.
More softly than the dew is shed,
Or cloud is floated overhead,
He giveth His belovèd, sleep.

Aye, men may wonder while they scan
A living, thinking, feeling man
Confirmed in such a rest to keep;
But angels say, and through the word
I think their happy smile is *heard*—
'He giveth His belovèd, sleep.'

For me, my heart that erst did go
Most like a tired child at a show,
That sees through tears the mummers leap,
Would now its wearied vision close,
Would child-like on His love repose,
Who giveth His belovèd, sleep.

And, friends, dear friends,—when it shall be
That this low breath is gone from me,
And round my bier ye come to weep,
Let One, most loving of you all,
Say, 'Not a tear must o'er her fall';
He giveth His belovèd, sleep.

Elizabeth Barrett Browning

IF MY BARK SINK

If my bark sink
'Tis to another sea.
Mortality's ground floor
Is immortality.

Emily Dickinson

333

"LEAF AFTER LEAF . . ."

Leaf after leaf drops off, flower after flower,
Some in the chill, some in the warmer hour:
Alike they flourish and alike they fall,
And earth who nourished them receives them all.
Should we, her wiser sons, be less content
To sink into her lap when life is spent?

Walter Savage Landor

EPITAPH

Even such is Time, which takes in trust
Our youth, our joys, and all we have,
And pays us but with age and dust,
Who in the dark and silent grave,
When we have wandered all our ways,
Shuts up the story of our days:
And from which earth, and grave, and dust,
The Lord shall raise me up, I trust.

Sir Walter Raleigh

AFTER WORK

Lord, when Thou seest that my work is done,
Let me not linger on,
With failing powers,
Adown the weary hours,—
A workless worker in a world of work.
But, with a word,
Just bid me home,
And I will come
Right gladly,—
Yea, right gladly
Will I come.

John Oxenham

334

UNTIL THE SHADOWS LENGTHEN

O Lord, support us all the day long
    of this troublous life,
Until the shadows lengthen,
And the evening comes,
And the busy world is hushed,
And the fever of life is over,
And our work is done.
Then of thy mercy
Grant us a safe lodging,
And a holy rest,
And peace at the last:
Through Jesus Christ our Lord. Amen.

John Henry Newman

TO PATHS UNKNOWN

When on my day of life the night is falling,
   And, in the winds from unsunned spaces blown,
I hear far voices out of darkness calling
   My feet to paths unknown,

Thou, who hast made my home of life so pleasant,
   Leave not its tenant when its walls decay:
O Love Divine, O Helper ever present,
   Be Thou my strength and stay!

Be near me when all else is from me drifting:
   Earth, sky, home's pictures, days of shade and shine,
And kindly faces to my own uplifting
   The love which answers mine.

I have but Thee, my Father! let Thy Spirit
   Be with me then to comfort and uphold;
No gate of pearl, no branch of palm I merit
   Nor street of shining gold.

335

Suffice it if—my good and ill unreckoned,
   And both forgiven through Thy abounding grace—
I find myself by hands familiar beckoned
   Unto my fitting place.

Some humble door among Thy many mansions,
   Some sheltering shade where sin and striving cease,
And flows forever through heaven's green expansions
   The river of Thy peace.

There, from the music round me stealing,
   I fain would learn the new and holy song,
And find at last, beneath Thy trees of healing,
   The life for which I long.

John Greenleaf Whittier

FROM *THE CHAMBERED NAUTILUS*

Build thee more stately mansions, O my soul,
      As the swift seasons roll!
      Leave thy low-vaulted past!
Let each new temple, nobler than the last,
Shut thee from heaven with a dome more vast,
      Till thou at length art free,
Leaving thine outgrown shell by life's unresting sea!

Oliver Wendell Holmes

PRAYER BEFORE HER EXECUTION

O merciful Father, my hope is in thee!
O Gracious Redeemer, deliver thou me!
My bondage bemoaning, with sorrowful groaning,
   I long to be free;

Lamenting, relenting, and humbly repenting,
O Jesu, my Saviour, I languish for thee!

Mary Queen of Scots

DAREST THOU NOW O SOUL

Darest thou now O soul,
Walk out with me toward the unknown region,
Where neither ground is for the feet nor any path to follow?

No map there, nor guide,
Nor voice sounding, nor touch of human hand,
Nor face with blooming flesh, nor lips, nor eyes, are in that
    land.

I know it not O soul,
Nor dost thou, all is a blank before us,
All waits undream'd of in that region, that inaccessible land.

Till when the ties loosen,
All but the ties eternal, Time and Space,
Nor darkness, gravitation, sense, nor any bounds bounding us.

Then we burst forth, we float,
In Time and Space O soul, prepared for them,
Equal, equipt at last, (O joy, O fruit of all) them to fulfill
    O soul.

Walt Whitman

MY AIN COUNTREE

I'm far frae my hame, an' I'm weary aftenwhiles,
For the langed-for hame-bringing
    an' my Father's welcome smiles;

I'll ne'er be fu' content, until my een do see
The shining gates o' heaven an' my ain countree.

The earth is flecked wi' flowers, mony-tinted, fresh an' gay,
The birdies warble blithely, for my Father made them sae;
But these sights an' these soun's will as naething be to me,
When I hear the angels singing in my ain countree.

I've his gude word of promise that some gladsome day the King
To his ain royal palace his banished hame will bring:
Wi' een an' wi' hearts runnin' ower we shall see
The King in his beauty in our ain countree.

My sins hae been mony, an' my sorrows hae been sair,
But there they'll never vex me, nor be remembered mair;
His bluid has made me white, his hand shall dry mine ee,
When he brings me hame at last to my ain countree.

Like a bairn to his mither, a wee birdie to its nest,
I wad fain be ganging noo unto my Saviour's breast;
For he gathers in his bosom, witless, worthless lambs like me,
An' he carries them himsel' to his ain countree.

He's faithfu' that hath promised, he'll surely come again;
He'll keep his tryst wi' me, at what hour I dinna ken:
But he bids me still to wait, an' ready aye to be,
To gang at ony moment to my ain countree.

So I'm watchin' aye, an' singin' o' my hame as I wait,
For the soundin' o' his footfa' this side the gowden gate,
God gie his grace to ilka ane what listens noo to me,
That we may a' gang in gladness to our ain countree.

Mary Demare

FROM *YOU CAN'T GO HOME AGAIN*

Something has spoken to me in the night, burning the tapers
of the waning year; something has spoken in the night, and told me
I shall die, I know not where. Saying:

*"To lose the earth you know, for greater knowing; to lose the
life you have, for greater life; to leave the friends you loved, for
greater loving; to find a land more kind than home, more large than
earth—*

*"—Whereon the pillars of this earth are founded, toward
which the conscience of the world is tending—a wind is rising,
and the rivers flow."*

Thomas Wolfe

AWAY

I cannot say, and I will not say
That he is dead. He is just away.

With a cheery smile, and a wave of the hand,
He has wandered into an unknown land.

And left us dreaming how very fair
It needs must be since he lingers there.

And you—O you, who the wildest yearn
For the old-time step and the glad return—

Think of him faring on, as dear
In the love of there as the love of here;

Think of him still as the same, I say;
He is not dead—he is just away!

James Whitcomb Riley

PROSPICE

Fear death?—to feel the fog in my throat,
    The mist in my face,
When the snows begin, and the blasts denote
    I am nearing the place,
The power of the night, the press of the storm,
    The post of the foe;
Where he stands, the Arch Fear in a visible form,
    Yet the strong man must go:
For the journey is done and the summit attained,
    And the barriers fall,
Though a battle's to fight ere the guerdon be gained,
    The reward of it all.
I was ever a fighter, so—one fight more,
    The best and the last!
I would hate that death bandaged my eyes, and forbore,
    And bade me creep past.
No! let me taste the whole of it, fare like my peers
    The heroes of old,
Bear the brunt, in a minute pay glad life's arrears
    Of pain, darkness and cold.
For sudden the worst turns the best to the brave,
    The black minute's at end,
And the elements' rage, the fiend-voices that rave,
    Shall dwindle, shall blend,
Shall change, shall become first a peace, then a joy,
    Then a light, then thy breast,
O thou soul of my soul! I shall clasp thee again,
    And with God be the rest!

Robert Browning

IN HIM

"We dwell in Him,"—oh, everlasting Home,
    Imperishable House not made with hands!

When all the world has melted as a dream,
    Eternal in the heav'ns this dwelling stands.

Annie Johnson Flint

WHEN ALL IS DONE

When all is done, and my last word is said,
And ye who loved me murmur, "He is dead,"
Let no one weep for fear that I should know,
And sorrow too that ye should sorrow so.

When all is done and in the oozing clay,
Ye lay this cast-off hull of mine away,
Pray not for me, for, after long despair,
The quiet of the grave will be a prayer.

For I have suffered loss and grievous pain,
The hurts of hatred and the world's disdain,
And wounds so deep that love, well-tried and pure,
Had not the pow'r to ease them or to cure.

When all is done, say not my day is o'er,
And that thro' night I seek a dimmer shore:
Say rather that my morn has just begun,—
I greet the dawn and not a setting sun,
        When all is done.

Paul Laurence Dunbar

FROM *THOMAS WOLFE'S TOMBSTONE*

THE LAST VOYAGE, THE LONGEST, THE BEST.
DEATH BENT TO TOUCH HIS CHOSEN SON
WITH MERCY, LOVE AND PITY,
AND PUT THE SEAL OF HONOR ON HIM
WHEN HE DIED.

Thomas Wolfe

341

DEATH, BE NOT PROUD

Death, be not proud, though some have callèd thee
Mighty and dreadful, for thou art not so;
For those whom thou think'st thou dost overthrow
Die not, poor Death; nor yet canst thou kill me.
From rest and sleep, which but thy pictures be,
Much pleasure; then from thee much more must flow;
And soonest our best men with thee do go—
Rest of their bones and souls' delivery!
Thou'rt slave to fate, chance, kings, and desperate men,
And dost with poison, war, and sickness dwell;
And poppy or charms can make us sleep as well
And better than thy stroke. Why swell'st thou then?
One short sleep past, we wake eternally,
And Death shall be no more: Death, thou shalt die.

John Donne

THE LAST INVOCATION

At the last, tenderly,
From the walls of the powerful fortress'd house,
From the clasp of the knitted locks, from the keep of the
    well-closed doors,
Let me be wafted.

Let me glide noiselessly forth;
With the key of softness unlock the locks—with a whisper,
Set ope the doors O soul.

Tenderly—be not impatient,
(Strong is your hold O mortal flesh,
Strong is your hold O love.)

Walt Whitman

342

EPITAPH

The Body
of
Benjamin Franklin
Printer
(Like the cover of an old book
Its contents torn out
And stript of its lettering and gilding)
Lies here, food for worms.
But the work shall not be lost
For it will (as he believed) appear once more
In a new and more elegant edition
Revised and corrected
by
The Author.

Benjamin Franklin

FROM *THANATOPSIS*

So live, that when thy summons comes to join
The innumerable caravan, which moves
To that mysterious realm, where each shall take
His chamber in the silent halls of death,
Thou go not, like the quarry-slave at night,
Scourged to his dungeon, but, sustained and soothed
By an unfaltering trust, approach thy grave,
Like one who wraps the drapery of his couch
About him, and lies down to pleasant dreams.

William Cullen Bryant

SAON OF ACANTHUS

Here lapped in hallowed slumber Saon lies,
Asleep, not dead; a good man never dies.

Callimachus (translated by J. A. Symonds)

343

THE CHARIOT

Because I could not stop for Death,
He kindly stopped for me;
The carriage held but just ourselves
And Immortality.

We slowly drove, he knew no haste,
And I had put away
My labour, and my leisure too,
For his civility.

We passed the school where children played,
Their lessons scarcely done;
We passed the fields of grazing grain,
We passed the setting sun.

We paused before a house that seemed
A swelling on the ground;
The roof was scarcely visible,
The cornice but a mound.

Since then 'tis centuries; but each
Feels shorter than the day
I first surmised the horses' heads
Were toward eternity.

Emily Dickinson

FROM *IN MEMORIAM*

The yule-clog sparkled keen with frost,
  No wing of wind the region swept,
  But over all things brooding slept
The quiet sense of something lost.

Alfred Tennyson

344

LIFE

Life! I know not what thou art,
But know that thou and I must part;
And when, or how, or where we met,
I own to me's a secret yet.
But this I know, when thou art fled,
Where'er they lay these limbs, this head,
No clod so valueless shall be
As all that then remains of me.

O whither, whither, dost thou fly?
Where bend unseen thy trackless course?
   And in this strange divorce,
Ah, tell where I must seek this compound I?
To the vast ocean of empyreal flame
   From whence thy essence came
Dost thou thy flight pursue, when freed
From matter's base encumbering weed?
   Or dost thou, hid from sight,
   Wait, like some spell-bound knight,
Through blank oblivious years th' appointed hour
To break thy trance and reassume thy power?
Yet canst thou without thought or feeling be?
O say, what art thou, when no more thou'rt thee?

Life! we have been long together,
Through pleasant and through cloudy weather;
   'Tis hard to part when friends are dear;
   Perhaps 'twill cost a sigh, a tear;—
   Then steal away, give little warning,
     Choose thine own time;
Say not Good-night, but in some brighter clime
     Bid me Good-morning!

Anna Laetitia Barbauld

FROM *RESIGNATION*

There is no Death. What seems so is transition;
 This life of mortal breath
Is but the suburb of the life elysian,
 Whose portal we call Death.

She is not dead,—the child of our affection,—
 But gone unto that school
Where she no longer needs our poor protection,
 And Christ Himself doth rule.

Henry Wadsworth Longfellow

GO DOWN, DEATH

Weep not, weep not,
She is not dead;
She's resting in the bosom of Jesus.
Heart-broken husband—weep no more;
Grief-stricken son—weep no more;
Left-lonesome daughter—weep no more;
She's only just gone home.

Day before yesterday morning,
God was looking down from his great, high heaven,
Looking down on all his children,
And his eye fell on Sister Caroline,
Tossing on her bed of pain.
And God's big heart was touched with pity,
With the everlasting pity.

And God sat back on his throne,
And he commanded that tall, bright angel standing at his
  right hand:
Call me Death!

346

And that tall, bright angel cried in a voice
That broke like a clap of thunder:
Call Death!—Call Death!
And the echo sounded down the streets of heaven
Till it reached away back to that shadowy place,
Where Death waits with his pale, white horses.

And Death heard the summons,
And he leaped on his fastest horse,
Pale as a sheet in the moonlight.
Up the golden street Death galloped,
And the hoofs of his horse struck fire from the gold,
But they didn't make no sound.
Up Death rode to the Great White Throne,
And waited for God's command.

And God said: Go down, Death, go down,
Go down to Savannah, Georgia,
Down in Yamacraw,
And find Sister Caroline.
She's borne the burden and heat of the day,
She's labored long in my vineyard,
And she's tired—
She's weary—
Go down, Death, and bring her to me.

And Death didn't say a word,
But he loosed the reins on his pale, white horse,
And he clamped the spurs to his bloodless sides,
And out and down he rode,
Through heaven's pearly gates,
Past suns and moons and stars;
On Death rode,
And the foam from his horse was like a comet in the sky;
On Death rode,
Leaving the lightning's flash behind;
Straight on down he came.

While we were watching round her bed,
She turned her eyes and looked away,
She saw what we couldn't see;
She saw Old Death. She saw Old Death,
Coming like a falling star.
But Death didn't frighten Sister Caroline;
He looked to her like a welcome friend.
And she whispered to us: I'm going home,
And she smiled and closed her eyes.

And Death took her up like a baby,
And she lay in his icy arms,
But she didn't feel no chill.
And Death began to ride again—
Up beyond the evening star,
Out beyond the morning star,
Into the glittering light of glory,
On to the Great White Throne.
And there he laid Sister Caroline
On the loving breast of Jesus.

And Jesus took his own hand and wiped away her tears,
And he smoothed the furrows from her face,
And the angels sang a little song,
And Jesus rocked her in his arms,
And kept a-saying: Take your rest,
Take your rest, take your rest.

Weep not—weep not,
She is not dead;
She's resting in the bosom of Jesus.

James Weldon Johnson

348

WAITING

Serene, I fold my hands and wait,
  Nor care for wind, or tide, or sea;
I rave no more 'gainst time or fate,
  For, lo! my own shall come to me.

I stay my haste, I make delays,
  For what avails this eager pace?
I stand amid the eternal ways,
  And what is mine shall know my face.

Asleep, awake, by night or day,
  The friends I seek are seeking me;
No wind can drive my bark astray,
  Nor change the tide of destiny.

What matter if I stand alone?
  I wait with joy the coming years;
My heart shall reap where it has sown,
  And garner up its fruit of tears.

The waters know their own and draw
  The brook that springs in yonder height;
So flows the good with equal law
  Unto the soul of pure delight.

The stars come nightly to the sky;
  The tidal wave unto the sea;
Nor time, nor space, nor deep, nor high,
  Can keep my own away from me.

John Burroughs

TO TOUSSAINT L'OUVERTURE

Toussaint, the most unhappy man of men!
    Whether the whistling Rustic tend his plough
    Within thy hearing, or thy head be now
Pillowed in some deep dungeon's earless den;—
O miserable Chieftain! where and when
    Wilt thou find patience? Yet die not; do thou
    Wear rather in thy bonds a cheerful brow:
Though fallen thyself, never to rise again,
Live, and take comfort. Thou hast left behind
    Powers that will work for thee; air, earth, and skies;
There's not a breathing of the common wind
    That will forget thee; thou hast great allies;
Thy friends are exultations, agonies,
    And love, and man's unconquerable mind.

William Wordsworth

ETERNAL LIFE

Those souls that of His own good life partake
He loves as His own Self; dear as His eye
They are to Him: He'll never them forsake.
When they shall die, then God Himself shall die!
They live, they live in blest eternity.

Henry More

GOD IS NIGH

Day is done, gone the sun
From the lake, from the hills, from the sky.
Safely rest, all is well! God is nigh.

Author unknown

INDEX OF SUBJECTS

INDEX FOR SPECIAL DAYS AND OCCASIONS

INDEX OF AUTHORS

Index of Authors

INDEX OF TITLES AND FIRST LINES

360

Index of Titles and First Lines

Index of Titles and First Lines

369